THE CLASSICS
OF WESTERN
SPIRITUALITY

THE CLASSICS OF WESTERN SPIRITUALITY
A Library of the Great Spiritual Masters

President and Publisher
Kevin A. Lynch, C.S.P.

EDITORIAL BOARD

Editor-in-Chief
John Farina

Angelus Silesius
THE CHERUBINIC WANDERER

TRANSLATION AND FOREWORD BY
MARIA SHRADY

INTRODUCTION AND NOTES BY
JOSEF SCHMIDT

PREFACE BY
E. J. FURCHA

PAULIST PRESS
NEW YORK • MAHWAH • TORONTO

Cover Art:

FREDERICK SHRADY, the eminent sculptor, has long been drawn to religious themes. The cover of this volume is concerned with the wayfarer's movement toward the eternal.

Among his most notable works are *St. Peter* at Lincoln Square, New York; *St. Elizabeth Seton* in St. Patrick's Cathedral and *The Virgin* in the Vatican Gardens.

Library of Congress
Catalog Card Number: 85-62963

ISBN: 0-8091-2768-7 (paper)
0-8091-0372-9 (cloth)

Published by Paulist Press
997 Macarthur Boulevard
Mahwah, New Jersey 07430

Printed and bound in the United States of America

Contents

Author of the Foreword and Translator of this Volume
MARIA SHRADY is the wife of the sculptor Frederick Shrady, the
mother of six children, and the author of *Come, Southwind, In the Spirit of
Wonder*, and *Moments of Insight*.

Author of the Introduction
JOSEF SCHMIDT is Associate Professor of German at McGill University in Montreal, Canada. After graduating from the monastery school in
Einsiedeln, Switzerland, he studied German, Greek and English in Salon-
ica (Greece), Edinburgh and Zurich where he received his Ph.D. in 1966.
Besides publishing numerous articles, he is also the author of several books:
one on German Jesuit theater and Jacob Böhme (1967), a standard anthology of sixteenth-century German literature (*Renaissance, Humanismus, Reformation*, [1976]) and a study of Reformation satire (1977). He was the
founding president of the Canadian Society for the History of Rhetoric.

Author of the Preface
EDWARD J. FURCHA is Associate Professor of Church History in the
Faculty of Religious Studies, Montreal. Among his publications are trans-
lations of works by Huldrych Zwingli, Hans Denck and Caspar von
Schwenckfeld. He is currently working on a translation of *Two Hundred
and Eighty Paradoxes* by Sebastian Franck.

Foreword

The Vision

Pure as the finest gold, hard as the granite stone,
Wholly as crystal clear your spirit must become. (1:1)

Within the narrowest frame the conditions that must precede the launching of the soul are indicated. Upon the firm foundation of this triad the cadence of the entire work is now allowed to rise. To understand it, we must be willing to meditate with Silesius, to bear with him when he repeats his fundamental ideas in rich variations. We must experience the ever-present attitude of speculative mysticism, its lofty voice, and its spirit of jubilant audacity. Under these conditions the effect will be liberating.

Angelus Silesius framed his thought in the most difficult form, the epigram, which by its tightness and brevity, enables the reader to grasp the point in a flash of recognition. Even when he wrote longer poems the whole of his thought is compressed into succinct configurations that etch themselves into the mind. With him, Alexandrine verse—usually associated with the hard, rational type of French poetry—has a compelling élan, a jubilant rhythm, perfectly suited to the tone of prophetic certainty. This poetry is not an external, artificial form, but the very essence of the thought. Image and thought are fused into one. Awareness of God is richly expressed in dramatic images which touch, slip, and slide into each other and frequently by a sudden and unexpected turn cancel each other out. Much use is made of metaphors, images pointing to the ineffable.

> I am a peak in God and must myself ascend
> If ever I be shown the dearest countenance. (2:83)

In speaking of God, Silesius is carried away by enthusiasm; he speaks from the depth of his soul. His imagination is inexhaustible in paradoxes:

> No future and no past! What is about to be
> Forever was in God perceived essentially. (2:182)

He employs concepts that seem contradictory. Employed as means of thinking the unthinkable, grasping that which cannot be grasped, they often negate themselves. This is inevitable and appropriate when thought invites failure by trying to express what is beyond thought:

> Where is my dwelling place? Where I can never stand.
> Where is my final goal, toward which I should ascend?
> It is beyond all place. What should my quest then be?
> I must, transcending God, into a desert flee. (1:7)

Far from being merely extravagant statements, these paradoxes become meaningful when considered within the framework of Silesius' vision. Let us attempt to disclose the meaning of that vision. Union of the soul with the Godhead and the harmony of all things in the divine Ground are the supreme goals of his poetic endeavor. All else—and there seems to be no mystery to which he has not addressed himself—is subordinated to those ideas. Once the soul gains awareness that its core is indestructible, and in its deepest ground identical with God, this awareness gives it a wonderful serenity. If the soul can know and unfold it, nothing in the world can affect it. Silesius never ceased to dwell on this in *The Cherubinic Wanderer*. Like a musical composition it develops infinite richness from a few themes. The basso ostinato is the need to transcend our conceptual thinking of God.

Strictly speaking, God is neither this nor that. In point of essence, nothing we say about Him is appropriate:

> The more you know of God, the more you will confess
> That what He is Himself, you can name less and less. (5:41)

FOREWORD

He is for us the hidden God, *Deus absconditus*, or, in the Classic Greek term, *Akataleptos*, the Incomprehensible. "He is dwelling in a light unapproachable, whom no man has seen or can see" (1 Tm 6:16). This is the mystery of Divine Transcendence. Again and again Silesius warns us to make sure that when we are thinking and speaking about God, it is really about God we are thinking and speaking:

> God far exceeds all words that we can here express
> In silence He is heard, in silence worshiped best. (1:240)

We cannot, as it were, crowd God into a concept. "If you have comprehended," St. Augustine said, "What you have comprehended is not God." When we think of God it is in categories without which no thinking is possible. But since He is subject to no categories, we must shatter them by thinking beyond them. We must, he says, remove from Him all similarity to the corporal and spiritual world as we know them:

> Most perfect purity is image-, form-, and love-less,
> Defies all attribute, as much as does God's essence. (2:70)

But even that is not enough. As the final step we remove from Him that very is-ness, as it is found in creatures:

> The tender Godhead is a naught and more than naught;
> Who nothing sees in all, believe me, he sees God. (1:111)

It is by this ignorance, as long as this life lasts, that we are best united to God, but this ignorance is knowledge, and this silence the language of adoration:

> Silence, Beloved, be still; if you be wholly quiet,
> God will show you more good than you know how to desire. (2:8)

This is more than an invitation to mere attentiveness, more than a summons to quiet thinking. With these words Silesius points to the realm of inwardness where we hope to gain access to God. Thus the *via negationis* of the theologian, which stated that in this life "We are united to God as to one unknown" (Aquinas), is analogous to the *via negativa* of mystical tradition which seeks to attain God in "the dazzling darkness of that silence which revealeth in secret" (Dionysius the Pseudo Areopagite). Here the experience of the mystic converges with the biblical exhortation "be still and know that I am God." Once the spirit has penetrated that inmost cell of silence, it can intercept the mysterious accents of the Word:

> The voice of God is heard: Listen within and seek;
> Were you but always silent, he'd never cease to speak. (5:330)

In silence the Eternal Word came down from Heaven, and only in silence can it be heard again. Eternally, God utters a single word:

> No one speaks less than God outside of time and place;
> He makes eternally a single utterance. (4:129)

This uttering of the Word is, in the language of speculative mysticism, "The Birth of the Son," and everything depends on this *mysterium tremendum* being effected in the secret spring of the soul:

> The Virgin I must be and bring God forth from me,
> Should ever I be granted divine felicity. (1:23)

What is the impulse behind so bold and perilous a statement? In order to understand it we must go back to Meister Eckhart, who propounded the idea in its purest form. Perhaps it can be summed up as follows: Eternally God speaks, utters the Son and in Him utters all things. We call this emergence of the Son the Eternal Generation from the Father. It happens without ceasing in the Eternal Now. In and with the Son, God utters the entire Universe, not the temporal-spatial one, but a spiritual, eternal one of which ours is merely a copy (1:108). This archetypal universe the Father contemplates in the Logos, which is Christ. He loves it in his Son, and the universe returns this love by ardently yearning toward its origin. What happens now to the temporal-spatial world, the world in which we live, struggle, and die? It would be a nothing, were it not related to the Eternal World of the Son (1:109). There it has its essence; outside of it, "it is not" (2:30). Hence the urge to ascend; to return to the sole reality pervades all creation.

But how is this return to be effected? Here we turn to man himself. In his highest and most noble faculties he is the image of God. The image stands in a living relation to the original. Where? At the point where the highest faculties of the soul have their source, in the ground of the soul. Here man is given to himself (1:6). But just as the seeing eye can see everything except itself, so the soul cannot conceive of itself. The source of its most secret self is hidden in darkness. This dazzling darkness, however, is where God acts (1:64). There, "God is greening and blooming with all His Godhead and its Spirit" (Meister Eckhart). Here the soul is touched by God, and man is given the freedom to let the uttering of the Word occur in him (5:249). In order for this to happen the soul must be totally abandoned. And having freed itself from all the beguilements of sense perception, it will be taken up into that movement which is the Eternal Birth of the Son and the resulting outpouring of the Spirit. It is in this active meeting and loving embrace that man's highest blessedness consists.

This process has enormous consequences. First, the ground of the soul becomes the holiest site in the universe. Whatever enters, whatever is recognized and loved, is already on its way to eternalization (1:193). Thus the destiny of creation is in the hands of man:

> Man, creatures love you so, it's you they are pressing toward;
> Hastening to come to you, thus to attain their God. (1:275)

This restitution of the world into its divine origin, from exteriority to interiority, from multiplicity into unity, is mediated by man:

> If you possess your God, all else will follow suit,
> Man, angel, sun and moon, air, fire, earth, and brook. (5:110)

Thus that great cyclic movement of all things from the Father back to the Father has been completed.

With equal passion the thinking of Silesius can do both: it effects the transcending which is forever propelled beyond itself, and in the bodily Christ and in the Church it accepts the revealed grace of God who turns to man in His Incarnation (3:1). To consider one without the other is to obscure his overall conception. Accepting the doctrines of the Church and living wholly within it, he nevertheless thought in such a way that the Christian content of his thought came to him as a consequence of his own speculation. Although he invokes the authority of Scripture, it is the force of his own vision that is total and overpowering:

> See, how God honors me! Leaping from His high throne,
> He places me upon it, in His beloved Son. (1:202)

The Johannine doctrine of divine filiation seems to merge with the Pauline claim that "we are of His kin." The metaphors used are dynamic relations, the bringing of a life of perceptions through a leap of recognition. This technique enables him to achieve the most astonishing condensation of otherwise complicated movements of thought. His trinitarian speculations are based on Scripture (Rom 11:36, 1 Cor 1:16) and rooted in the Greek doctrine of *Synkephaloisis*, which states that the Three are One because the Father, the *archê*, is the source from Whom they come and into Whom they are again gathered:

> The Godhead is a source from which all things do rush,
> And then return to it. An ocean it is thus. (3:168)

In all a single impulse is at work: the soul's drive toward its source in that great wheeling movement which is energized by love. Although the word "love" can take on innumerable meanings, it has lost none of its force and weight:

> Love reigns as Sovereign; even the Trinity
> To love submissive is throughout eternity. (5:241)

Of this love every other love is a copy; or, in other words, every other love finds its consummation in the love of God:

> The beauty of the creature is nothing but a bridge,
> Which leads to the Creator, Who Himself Beauty is. (3:102)

What keeps love from being ambiguous is its final criterion:

> Tell me where love is found in her most cherished place?
> Where to the Cross she is bound, for the Beloved's sake. (5:28)

The same thought, taken an interval higher, results in a paradox of incomparable pathos:

> Love like a magnet is, it draws me into God,
> And what is greater still, it pulls God into death. (2:2)

It is in such terms that Angelus Silesius speaks of love. Throughout all his speculations he never loses sight of his final goal which is divinization (1:124). The term, which to many has proved a stumbling block, is classic with the Greek Fathers, particularly with Athanasius: "The Son of God became son of man"; so he writes, "so that the sons of man, that is of Adam, might become Sons of God. Thus he is Son of God by nature, and we by grace" (*De incarn. et contra Ar.* 8). And Cyril of Alexandria sums up: "We are made partakers of divine nature and are said to be sons of God, nay we are actually called divine, not only because we are exalted by grace to supernatural glory, but also because we have God dwelling in us" (in Jn 1). This is the orbit in which Silesius moved, marked out by the ideas of participation in the divine nature (the purity of which he never tired of exalting), rebirth through the Spirit, adoption as Sons—all concepts leading to deification (6:234) and expressed with depth and boldness and sublime inwardness.

The poems of *The Cherubinic Wanderer* present the crystallization of centuries of collective thought, ranging from Plato and Plotinus across Augustine and the Pseudo Areopagite directly to Eckhart and the school of German speculative mysticism. We may be tempted to ask: What, then, is really new? What is decisively new is the whole with its impulsions, its vision, the way in which the poet made it his own, the context and the emphasis. His work contains the themes of the Philosophia Perennis, shaped by a man who knew how to elucidate speculative truths in a unique way. At moments, certain of his ideas seem to burst the bonds of discursive thought: It is then that his insights set off flashes of lightning and we, too, participate for an instant in his vision, which imparts a timeless knowledge of Being. In an age in which men seek transcendence under new conditions this vision still serves as an orientation.

Preface

With the recent revival of interest in mysticism, both East and West, Christian and other, concern with specific exponents of mystical ideas has naturally been rekindled. An anthology of the best spiritual verses of Johann Scheffler, better known as Angelus Silesius, one of the great German mystics of the seventeenth century, is therefore not only a desideratum but, indeed, a must.

Maria Shrady, Josef Schmidt, and the editor-in-chief of The Classics of Western Spirituality deserve high commendation for their willingness to introduce to a largely North American readership these "gems" of an almost forgotten German whose aphorisms speak of the divine-human encounter in language that elevates the spirit and invites reflection on the meaning of life even as it transcends the mundane and ordinary.

Johann Scheffler was born in Wroclaw (Breslau), Poland, in 1624, the very year in which Jakob Böhme, mystic, brilliant autodidact, and cobbler, died in his native Goerlitz. It was the year in which another great person, George Fox of Quaker fame, was born. These two were bright luminaries in the heaven of "inner religion" whose radiance was to brighten dark paths of pilgrims of hope for generations to come.

Scheffler came of a family of Lutheran "dissidents." His father was a landholder who had "retired" to Wroclaw to escape persecution for his Lutheran convictions. Johann was privileged enough to enjoy the best education that could be offered. After high school he traveled to Strasbourg to study medicine, a pursuit he continued in Padua. During his student days he spent some time in Holland (Amsterdam and Leiden), where he was first exposed to the writings of Jakob Böhme. After his doctorate in medicine and philosophy, earned in 1648, he returned to his homeland to work as a private physician of Count Sylvius Nimrod ef Wuerttemberg-Oels. During these years, Scheffler maintained a close friendship with Franckenberg, a friend of Böhme, whose "heretical" ideas were widely known. At the same time, relationships with the orthodox Lutherans at the court, especially with the court chaplain, became strained.

Not surprisingly, Scheffler left the employ of the count and returned to Wroclaw where in 1653 he converted to Roman Catholicism. At this time he adopted the name Johann Angelus, after a Spanish mystic of the sixteenth century. Henceforth he published his mystical writings and his poetry under the name Angelus Silesius, though his polemical writings of later years—often vitriolic and in no way conciliatory—continued to appear under his former name.

Though Scheffler lived a relatively short life (he died in 1677, aged fifty-three), he established himself as physician, theologian, poet, and priest of the Roman Catholic Church. In the latter capacity he had become an ardent advocate of the so-called Counter-Reformation and generally suspect by Protestants.

Though Scheffler's mystical writings are not original but often "recreations" of those of earlier mystics, notably Jakob Böhme, he was widely read in his own day. Indeed, later generations found their way back to his inspirational verse. The historian Gottfried Arnold, a Lutheran pietist, admired his *Cherubinic Wanderer* so greatly that he published it in 1701. Friedrich Schlegel rediscovered him for the nineteenth century and August Kahlert wrote one of the most exhaustive biographies of Scheffler in 1853, which was to be followed by later editions of his collected works. Ellinger in the twentieth century considers *The Cherubinic Wanderer* a superb piece of mystical writing, one that is not "exclusively catholic" but echoes strains of pantheist and spiritualist thought.

What makes Angelus Silesius attractive once again and appealing even to a North American readership? Three factors might be cited. Though these could be claimed for persons like Jakob Böhme or the great medieval mystic Meister Eckhart, they apply specifically to the best of Scheffler's spiritual verse and his numerous hymns, which exude a serenity that characterized this rather intense man.

The first factor is the spiritual detachment of a brilliant mind, capable of reaping all the benefits education, preferment, and social or ecclesiastical structures can offer without allowing them to dwarf the life of the spirit. In fact, Scheffler is able to shun them for the "simple" life of the spirit in *imitatio Christi* and in keeping with the life-style of primitive Christianity. This spells discipleship and genuine pilgrimage to a greater and richer dimension of life. Mystics before and after him have used the term *Gelassenheit* for the state of surrender to the will of God and have described the spiritual journey as stages upward or inward toward union with God.

A second factor, closely related to the first yet quite distinct, is the poet's search for meaning in a world of confusing signals and conflicting value systems. Undoubtedly not unaffected by the ravages of the Thirty Years War—the last major religious conflict among European nations—Scheffler finds meaning in poetry that does not escape doubt but transforms the dark nights of the soul through "purity of spirit," participation in the "light supreme" or in the "new birth"—an eternal reshaping of that which is truly human into that which is wholly divine.

A third factor in Scheffler's life work—though greatly obscured by the angry outpourings against expressions of Protestant dissent, as if he were somehow avenging his childhood hurts by now joining the persecutors and becoming one himself—is an "ecumenism of ecclesiastical uniformity," which Scheffler espouses in the highly polemical anti-Protestant pamphlets he published from 1661 onward. While these are not unimportant in an effort to understand this complex person, they cannot concern us here.

We must briefly return to Scheffler's poetry. Several of his hymns are still favorites and are to be found in Protestant hymnbooks. They express inner strength and exude the confidence of a life of faith. Though they reflect a Jesus mysticism that borders on the erotic, they speak eloquently of the inner life of a person who has come to knowledge of the divine through experience and not through learning. The poet speaks of the love of Jesus by which the yearning soul is saved. His best hymns compare favorably with those of his contemporary Paul Gerhard.

While only specialists would want to turn to his polemical tracts, seekers of all faiths or none may find in his hymns and above all in his *Cherubinic Wanderer* a path to the abyss of spiritual encounter with the divine at the core of which the seeker is set free from anxiety and enabled to be attuned to the source of life that makes creative living possible in the face of death

PREFACE

and potential annihilation. There one discovers the center of the unity of life that breaks down barriers of language, race, creed, or color; there one encounters the living God whose altars are not made of stone but inscribed on the heart of believing persons whose very ground is thus firmly anchored.

Translator's Note

The present translation was made from the authoritative edition by Hans Ludwig Held which is based on the Editio Princeps (Vienna 1657) and on the second edition (Glatz 1675), to which Silesius had added a sixth book. Although I have attempted to render an exact version of a difficult text, I am not unaware of Wilhelm von Humboldt's strictures on translation: "To say hippos, equus, and horse is not to say exactly and thoroughly the same thing." The "Wanderer" is composed in rhymed Alexandrine verse, and we must remember that German is rich in rhyme that frequently falls into place more readily than in English. But after all distinctions are allowed for, the fact remains that English is not so alien to the original text of Silesius that it could not be rendered with felicity. Accordingly, I have used rhyme and consonance proved fitting in those cases in which it did not violate the music of the verse. On the whole, too much euphony has been avoided since an overly smooth readability robs this poetry of its particular zest, and as a result the grainy texture dissolves in the air, allowing the spiritual energy to escape. In a very few cases dissonance seemed to actually heighten the pathos of the subject matter, (see 2:2), at least to our modern sensibilities. Surprisingly, a small amount of latinized vocabulary, inevitable in English, achieved remarkably beautiful effects of contrast by the close juxtaposition of one- or two-syllable Anglo-Saxon words with those of Latin origin. In perhaps the most beautiful of all his poems—the fourteen-line lyric entitled "How God dwells in the Holy Soul"—this interplay may be noticed in the eleventh line: "And like the oil of cinammon ignited." Here the last two words, placed among the simple Anglo-Saxon syllables of the preceding and following lines, give a sense of color and mystery to the whole poem. Thus, occasionally, the exigencies of the verse imposed on the translator may turn into blessings, as long as extreme accuracy of meaning is observed and none of the shape and movement of metered language is lost.

Finally, the question has been raised whether the selection made from a choice of 1,676 couplets, quatrains, and short poems is "oriented." The question does not strike me as very fruitful. Oriented toward what? It is indeed possible to arrive at various tendentious readings of Silesius by making him sound like Lao-Tse (2: 209), or again by robbing him of all audacity and paradox in concentrating on the didactic, catechetical verses. Another criterion would be the sheer musical quality of those lines that lend themselves most readily to translation. All these approaches, however, do a disservice to the poet by limiting the totality of his vision, of which the *Cherubinic Wanderer* is a unique distillation. For only by touching all the strings, are the sanity and the balance, the unity and the consistency of this intellectual poetry allowed to securely vibrate.

Introduction*

*I am indebted to Douglas Hall, John Hellman, and Robert Sullivan for helpful criticism. Except for verses from *The Cherubinic Wanderer* which are presented in Maria Shrady's translation, all other translations from German and Latin are mine unless otherwise noted.

The Cherubinic Wanderer is, according to the standard history of German literature, one of only two poetic texts from the Baroque age that have remained alive in their own culture.[1] Although its author, Johannes Scheffler (later called Angelus Silesius), spent the latter part of his life as a garrulous confessional polemicist, this sublime work of profound spirituality has transcended the (Catholic) confessional boundaries and enjoyed equal appreciation by different family members of the Christian church. In our time, the eminent theologian Hans Urs von Balthasar edited a selection of couplets as a book of contemplative prayer and praised the work for its powerful immediacy of devotional expression, which could appeal directly to a modern Christian.[2] On the other hand, many of the couplets of this work, taken out of context, can appeal to a modern reader as poetic versions of key concepts of existential philosophy—like the last part of Martin Heidegger's *Vom Wesen des Grundes* (On the essence of the reason, 1929). Because of the many levels of devotional expression, *The Cherubinic Wanderer* has also permeated popular culture in that many verses have become an integral part of German Christmas folklore. In our time, a sophisticated author like Umberto Eco in his bestseller *The Name of the Rose* (1980), a semiotic detective story set in a late medieval monastery at the time of the great schism, uses a particularly enigmatic couplet (1:25) to challenge the reader on the very last page. In the English-speaking world, this mystical text has become known to only a limited readership; in fact, even the name of the author is missing in

---

1. Richard Newald, *Vom Späthumanismus bis zur Empfindsamkeit, 1570–1750* (5, München, 1967), *Geschichte der deutschen Literatur* (Bd. 5), ed. R. Newald and H. de Boor, 261. The second work is the picaresque novel *Simplicissimus* by Johannes Ch. von Grimmelshausen. The authoritative edition is the one of Hans Ludwig Held (cf. note 4, Bd. 3, Munchen, 1949). An inexpensive modernized pocketbook edition with an instructive preface is the *Goldmann-Edition* (No. 607, München, 1960) by Charles Woldemar. The most recent historical-critical edition was done by Louise Gnädinger (Stuttgart: Reclam, 1984).

2. *Dich auftun wie die Rose*, *Sigillum* 2 (Einsiedeln, 1954).

that great pioneering classic on mystical spirituality, Evelyn Underhill's *Mysticism* (1910).[3]

1. Life

Johann Scheffler was born at the end of December 1624, in the Silesian capital of Breslau. The Thirty Years War had unleashed its devastating violence seven years before, and Scheffler was to be twenty-three before the Treaty of Westphalia reestablished the old order in continental Europe. Silesia was particularly ravaged by marauding troops, summary executions, and physical destruction that decades of changing alliances had brought about. However, even after the peace of 1648, the province continued to be a hotbed of bitter controversy. The House of Hapsburg had tried to forcefully re-catholicize a region that had a unique history of religious strife, for it was here that the enthusiasts and Anabaptists had survived both Lutheran and Catholic persecution. Scheffler's year of birth coincided with the end of the life of the most influential mystic in the wider context of this tradition: Jakob Böhme.

Even though we know the facts about Scheffler's adult life fairly well, there is a peculiar absence of almost any kind of direct testimony about the major motives determining his spiritual development.[4] If, however, one views his biography from a greater distance—transcending the historical and geographical data that mark his career as a Lutheran physician, and later as a Catholic priest—there is an astonishing congruence with the fundamental splendor, the dynamics, contradictions, discrepancies, and enigmas of his time. His life reflects the agonies that the Counter-Reformation caused to individuals, communities, and whole regional cultures. The urge for representation manifested itself in a most provocative public display of devotion overshadowing a pure and dedicated personal religious conviction. Scheffler's personal charity and asceticism contrasted

---

3. (New York: Scarborough, 1974).
4. All biographical presentations draw heavily from the first vol. 1 (A.S., Die Geschichte seines Lebens und seiner Werke; Urkunden) of Hans Ludwig Held's edition *Angelus Silesius, Sämtliche poetische Werke* (3. Aufl., München, 1952). This edition offers a wide choice of original texts and documents. It is based on the exemplary edition of Georg Ellinger (1895), who did the pioneering research and who published a separate biography (*Ein Lebensbild*) in 1927. The American monograph by Jeffrey Sammons in the *Twayne World Author Series* (25, New York, 1967) is an excellent introduction that is naturally oriented toward the literary aspect of Scheffler and his work. The latest article presenting new findings is Louise Gnädinger's "Angelus Silesius," in *Deutsche Dichter des 17. Jahrhunderts*, hrsg. v. Harald Steinhagen und Benno v. Wiese et al. (Berlin, 1984), 553–575.

sharply with his vitriolic outbursts of hate as a confessional polemicist; sublime mystical insights would give way to scornful triumphalist tirades in confessional battles. He played a very active part in the re-catholicization of his native city, yet at the same time joined the publicistic fight against the Turks, who were not only threatening Vienna, the Hapsburg capital, but also rivaling the Christian faith after emerging from another world religion's attempt at expansion, His *Cherubinic Wanderer*, however, remains a work of pure and lucid mystical insight, free from the excesses and the controversy that were to determine a sizable part of his life; it is truly a testimony of the rejuvenating forces that emerged in the Catholic Church in the course of the Counter-Reformation.

Youth and early adulthood seem to hold the key to explaining three distinctive features in Scheffler's biography: a need to identify with institutions, an openness for friendship, and occasional fits of excessive behavior. He was born, the first of three children, to Stanislaus Scheffler, a Protestant nobleman of low rank, who, probably because of his religion, moved late in life from Cracow as Lord of Borwicz to Breslau in 1618. He led the life of a wealthy burgher and lent money at interest; through this activity—he had to be reprimanded by the city council for uncivil methods of money collecting—we have the scant pieces of information about his origin.[5] At the age of 62 he married a twenty-four-year-old girl, Maria Hennemann. Stanislaus Scheffler died in 1637 when his son Johannes was twelve years old, and in the spring of 1639 Johannes' mother passed away too, leaving behind Johannes, his sister and his brother, the last of whom became mentally ill soon thereafter. The family life, if we are to believe a few cryptic remarks, had probably been quite harsh and austere.[6] Scheffler received a humanist education at the renowned *Elisabethgymnasium;* the high educational standard was further raised when around this time the Jesuits started their activities in Breslau after a period of Protestant domination. Among the most influential people in Scheffler's life was one of his professors, Christian Köler (1602–1658), friend and biographer of Martin Opitz, the famous author of *The Book of German Poetics* (1624), the standard work for poets in the seventeenth century; a close school friend was Andreas Schultz (Scultetus, 1622–1647), who also introduced him to poetry and who later converted to Catholicism and joined a Jesuit novitiate.

Thanks to the money left by his parents, Scheffler could pursue his studies free of financial worry and did his university degree in a manner

---

5. Cf. Held, *Angelus Silesius,* 13ff.
6. Cf. Sammons, *Angelus Silesius,* 16f.

befitting a moderately wealthy gentleman. After a short stay in Strasbourg (1643) he transferred to the University of Leyden, a move that proved important for his later life. For it was here that he came into contact with people of a unique social mix. Persecution had made the Netherlands a haven for all kinds of minorities: Christian sectarians (e.g., Mennonites), Jews, and numerous lay communities dating back in their origins to pre-Reformation *devotio moderna*. Religious life outside the Church institutions flourished, and Amsterdam was undoubtedly the publishing center of European mysticism of that age. Because Scheffler later professed a very rigid adherence to Catholic orthodoxy, it is difficult to evaluate his claim of having only skimmed the surface of this strange new world. In spite of his assertions he must have witnessed the wide and extensive influence of various mystical movements, and we are fairly sure that it was here that he came into contact with Jakob Böhme's writings, particularly the *Aurora* (Day-dawning), which was to become so essential for his spiritual development.

In 1647, he left Leyden and that fall matriculated at the University of Padua. He received a combined M.D./Ph.D. in the summer of 1648. There is a statement from a later date interpreting his stay in Italy as a main factor leading to his conversion—but it has to be read with caution. He claimed that he had been overwhelmed by the beauty of Catholic liturgy and the popular forms of pious devotion, in particular the festive structure of the Church year, and that this started him on the path to both conversion and priesthood.[7] The twenty-five-year-old doctor returned to his native city no later than 1649 and received his inheritance from his guardians; in the summer of the same year he was appointed court physician by the ruler of the principality of Oels in Silesia, Duke Sylvius Nimrod of Württemberg (1622–1664). The Duke was a stern Lutheran; however, it was not his animosity but that of members of his court that made Scheffler quit his position soon after (December 1652).

During this time, a most fortuitous friendship was struck with a man of outstanding erudition and Christian faith, Abraham von Franckenberg (1593–1652), a wealthy nobleman who two years before his death had passed his wealth to his brother and now led an ascetic, withdrawn life in the ancestral castle. His fame today rests on his biography of Jakob Böhme, and the editions of several works (1642) of this mystic whose friend he had been. Franckenberg succeeded in preventing Scheffler from getting into all

---

7. This argument features prominently in the pamphlet justifying his conversion, published in 1653.

kinds of social difficulties. He was a man of many spiritual interests, particularly alchemy and mysticism, and he diligently maintained a nonconfessional stand in rather turbulent times. A poet of some merit, he introduced Scheffler to the habit of writing down insights in short, concise—even terse—form. It was during this time that substantial portions of the *Cherubinic Wanderer* were written.[8] We are well informed about this friendship because Franckenberg not only generously provided Scheffler with books—which introduced him to Johannes Tauler, the visions of St. Mechtild, St. Gertrud, and the revelations of St. Bridget of Sweden; he also willed his library to Scheffler, for whom this was "a true psychopharmakon."[9] Many of these books, above all the *Theologia Deutsch* of the Frankfurter, profoundly shaped Scheffler's future life and work. The connection with works of Giordano Bruno or some Cabbalistic authors remains more vague.

As a result of this *lectio divina*, Scheffler decided to publish a small selection of mystical texts that had impressed him deeply.[10] He was quite taken aback when he found himself hindered in this by the court preacher, a rigid Lutheran by the name of Christoph Freytag. Because Lutherans felt increasingly threatened by "enemies from within." (Calvinists, Schwenckfeldians, etc.), the chaplain, in his function as censor, denied the imprimatur on the basis of this booklet's possibly being an obstacle to the "smashing of the enthusiasts."[11] Apparently this was a calculated attack. Other members of Franckenberg's circle of friends had had frequent difficulties with Lutheran orthodoxy, but this was the first time that an open confrontation of this kind had happened to Scheffler, who could not understand the resistance to what he saw as a purely religious matter. He was not only frustrated but also disgusted—although he later tried to minimize the importance of this incident as a possible motivating force for his decision to convert to Catholicism. Around this time he started to read St. Ignatius's *Exercises;* he also commenced a spiritual diary in the manner of the Jesuits; this book was found after his death (*libellus desideriorum Ioannis Amati*) but, unfortunately, has not been preserved.

The scandal this instance of censorship caused has to be understood against the historical background. Apparently, Scheffler was by now fairly

---

8. Cf. Guy-Marie Oury, *Chercher Dieu dans sa Parole; la lectio divina* (Chambray-les-Tours, 1982), which is an excellent introduction to the "practices" of devotion that Scheffler had adopted from a monastic perspective.

9. Cf. Held, *Angelus Silesius*, 28.

10. Sammons, *Angelus Silesius*, 25.

11. Ibid., 24f.

well known in the region. Re-catholicization of Silesia, where imperial (Catholic) doctrine was imposed on a largely Protestant population that reacted with but lukewarm fervor, save such occurences more prominence than they otherwise would have had. Religious infighting took place at many institutional levels: schools, courts, municipal offices; and the rift steadily worsened. Half a year after the denial of permission to publish, Scheffler converted to Catholicism in the St. Matthias church (June 12, 1653), took the name Angelus (the Silesius was added to distinguish him from a Lutheran preacher bearing this name), and with the proselytizing zeal of a convert did everything to lend credence to Lutheran charges of opportunism and heresy that were emerging at a rapid pace. His publication of "Fundamental Causes and Motives Why He Left Lutheranism and Professed the Catholic Church," published simultaneously in Olmütz and the renowned Jesuit college town of Ingolstadt in 1653, is divided into two sets of arguments, pro and contra. The twenty arguments against Lutheranism, however, do not argue the theological substance of Lutheran theology, but rather follow the well-established vituperative pattern of four generations of Catholic apologetic authors, first developed by Cochlaeus and "perfected" by Johannes Pistorius in his *Anatomiae Lutheri*.[12] Emphasis is on an *argumentum ad hominem* basis, in that the person rather than the ideas is discredited. The attempt is made to quote contradictory statements of the reformer and thus make him (and his descendants) appear foolish and unsavory. After the publication of this tract, Scheffler was granted an appointment as Royal Imperial Court Physician by Ferdinand III, an honorary title that did, however, carry tangible tax benefits. From this date, the floodgates of insolent accusations and counter-accusations remained wide open.

Scheffler found a new friend in a position of authority, Sebastian von Rostock (1607–1671), the vicar general and chief administrator of the Counter-Reformation in Breslau. Von Rostock later became Prince-Bishop (1664); he was an extremely aggressive church dignitary who alienated many by preaching re-catholicization of Silesia and simultaneously pursuing a policy of quickly reclaiming former church property and property to which the church might have a claim according to the stipulations of the Treaty of Westphalia. The vicar eagerly prompted Angelus Silesius to become a full-time publicist for his causes. Von Rostock was also a censor, and when he gave Scheffler the imprimatur for his two major works, *The*

---

12. The three books were published by Arnold Quentel in Cologne (1595) and served as the standard source of vituperation against Luther right into the twentieth century.

INTRODUCTION

Cherubinic Wanderer and *The Holy Joy of the Soul,* he must have known what
this meant as compensation for the shock Scheffler received when the Lutheran court denied permission to have his mystical anthology printed. He
engaged the help of the most prominent Jesuit dramatist of that time, Nicolaus Avancini (1612–1683) of Vienna, who looked after the publication
of the more subtle (and potentially controversial) *Cherubinic Wanderer* while
the "safe" *Holy Joy,* with its lucid and acceptable Jesuit orientation, could
be published in Scheffler's native city.

When exactly Scheffler did write the poems that were first published
in 1657 (only five books) is not certain. Angelus Silesius claims that he
started with a creative outburst (Preface to the 1675 edition) in the early
fifties when he wrote more than three hundred couplets during a period of
only four days. A supporting factor for this claim—an early genesis of the
first five books—can be seen in his acquaintance around that time (1651–
1652) with a friend of Franckenberg's whose epigrams are of equal mystical
orientation and quality, Daniel Czepko von Reigersfeld (1605–1660); his
Sexcenta monodisticha sapientium (written between 1648 and 1655) influenced
Scheffler directly.

Information on Scheffler's life after the conversion can be inferred
from several acts and incidents brought to light either in legal documents
or in the pamphlets of the publicistic battle in which he was engaged. On
the one hand he committed himself to genuine acts of charity, be it as godfather for poor children, dispenser of alms, or donator of pious foundations
devoted to the establishment of religious rites—he went so far as to sign
away most of his inheritance for charitable purposes. He lived frugally and
in a most committed ascetic way. But on the other hand he displayed ostentatious forms of devotion and adoration that had an undoubtedly provocative character. For example, when certain forms of processions were
readmitted, he took part in them in a demonstrative manner reminiscent
of the flagellants of earlier times, castigating himself and shocking the not
so discriminating sensibilities of his contemporaries.

In 1661 Scheffler was ordained a priest. From 1664 to 1666, through
the patronage of Sebastian von Rostock, he held the position of court marshal at the Prince-Bishop's residence. Von Rostock had been instrumental
in bringing the Jesuits back to Silesia when it was not quite legal to do so,[13]

---

13. As an example of how powerful the Jesuits' thrust was, cf. Jean Delumeau's *Catholicism between Luther and Voltaire: A New View of the Counter-Reformation* (London/Philadelphia, 1977), 34. At the time of Ignatius's death (1556), the company totalled 1,000 members.
At the time of the publication of *The Cherubinic Wanderer* there were 15,000 members, 550
foundations, and a total of 150,000 students. Contrary to traditional opinion, the Jesuits seem

and this might have been one of the reasons he aided Scheffler (who was not a Jesuit) so actively in responding to ever shriller polemical publications. Scheffler started to write on everything from traditional warnings against the Turks (1663; they were threatening to lay siege to Vienna) to admonitions to be generous when making property settlements with the church. However, being a man of single-minded determination, he fanatically pursued this road when even Catholic bishops joined Lutheran critics and (in 1664) tried to get an injunction at the Imperial Diet in order to silence this extreme zealot. About this time, some signs of tolerance surfaced, probably stemming from a general weariness about the futility of confessional efforts to win the heart of Christians of both denominations by violent or juridical means. But these signs went unheeded by Scheffler, who was increasingly hated by his enemies.

Scheffler undermined his health by working tirelessly for what he believed to be the good of the church. His dispirited isolation shows in the preface to the *Ecclesiologia*, a collection of thirty-nine of his more telling pamphlets for the cause. Even such a moderate critic as Hans Urs von Balthasar finds this work rather mediocre and without distinctive stylistic or theological profile.[14] A Jesuit priest, Daniel Schwartz, held an unusually warm eulogy on the occasion of Scheffler's interment. Selfless charity and devotion are praised. But *The Cherubinic Wanderer*, whose second and enlarged edition had appeared in 1675, is not even mentioned in this *oraison funebre;* it was, however, cherished by a devout readership of the faithful of later generations. Nonetheless, when Erdmann Neumeister published the authoritative register of baroque German authors toward the end of the century (*Survey of German Literature of our Age*, 1695), Angelus Silesius merited only a brief entry. Later generations began to appreciate the beauty of this splendid work that, in a following section, will be set against the literary background of the time.[15]

---

to have established a high school in Breslau by 1638 (cf. Wilfried Barner, *Barockrhetorik. Untersuchungen zu ihren geschichtlichen Grundlagen* [Tübingen, 1970]) 324–25.

14. Cf. von Balthasar, 101.

15. In my biographical sketch, I have drawn mainly from Gnädinger and Sammons. Günter Grass, in his novel *The Meeting in Telgte* (1979; American translation London/New York: Harcourt Brace Jovanovich, 1981), portrays Angelus Silesius in a rather spirited parody; cf. chapter 11 and *passim*.

2. The Epigrammatic Tradition

The epigrammatic couplet is the dominant form used in *The Cherubinic Wanderer*. A concise poetic and historical reflection on the genre might aid in a proper understanding of this mystical text.

The epigram was a favorite form of expression for humanistic sagacity in the sixteenth and seventeenth centuries. In both Latin and the vernacular, any imaginable topic could be treated using various types of verses as couplets or quadruplets. The humanist arch-poetics, Scaliger's *Poetices Libri Septem* (1561), contain a description of the salient features of this well-established genre. The chief characteristics are brevity and terse pointedness (argutia; III, CXXVI); its definition and functions are described as follows: "The epigram is thus a short poem dealing with a simple matter, a person, or an incident; or it can deduce something from given premises."[16] When Martin Opitz published his *Book of German Poetics* (1624), he expanded on this description by suggesting a variety of topics and assigning a function to the form.

The epigram is a short kind of satyre; for brevity is its chief feature and terse pointed sagacity its soul and form. The end is particularly significant in that it always turns out contrary to what we expect and is where the sharp wit is tied up. Even though the epigram can be used to cover any topic, it should be employed above all for love, for epitaphs of monuments and buildings, for the praise of noble men and women, witticisms and, of course, also for spiteful scorn and demasking of other people's weaknesses and vices.[17]

Opitz's normative description has been transcended by Angelus Silesius in his *Cherubinic Wanderer*. But the basic features, translated into a religious and even mystagogical (intentionally designed for mystical comprehension) context, are clearly the same. Before we proceed to analyze this, however, a short explanatory remark is in order. Most critics have depicted the learned tradition leading to this spiritual climax, but they have neglected to mention that one of the epigram's intrinsic qualities was that it was one of the few genres that was firmly rooted in both the Neo-Latin tradition and the popular traditions in the vernacular. Whatever the form—the proverb, the wise saying, the doggerel of a popular song—the short and concise

---

16. Quoted in Gerhard Neumann, *Deutsche Epigramme* (Stuttgart, 1969), 294.
17. Trans. from the authoritative German edition (Tübingen: Niemeyer, 1966), 21.

couplet served an identical function in popular culture in that it could cover a whole range of purposes from a short prayer to an obscene joke. German Baroque literature provides excellent examples of all these traditions.

Opitz, the arch-poet of German verse in the seventeenth century, praises the epigram for its condensed form, the sagacious possibilities for the poet, and the laconic brevity. These features made it a favorite of both Renaissance and the Baroque for it was beautifully suited for the main role of verse: occasional poetry. This meant that all aspects of life furnished opportunities for illumination through poetic exhortation—from birth to death, from brothel to monastic *ecstasis*.

The epigram developed its Baroque tradition in three main branches: a Neo-Latin tradition, a development in the vernacular of the various national cultures of Europe, and a popular tradition harnessed by attempts to tame doggerel with this sophisticated technique. It was an English poet, John Owen (1560–1622), whose eleven books of Latin epigrams became even more famous than the classical models of antiquity (above all, Martial). They were translated into German in 1653, the date of Scheffler's conversion to Catholicism. The learned tradition is best represented by the over 3,500 *Sinngedichte* (emblematic/allegorical verses) by Friedrich Logau (1604–1655), whose witty moralistic and satirical skill made the epigram truly fashionable among the learned poets of his age. The popular epigrams were most often anonymous; they surface in sermons, popular novels, refrains of folksongs, and so forth.

What is the bearing of this on Angelus Silesius's mystical texts? It shows that even in a narrow sense the poetic form had matured to a degree of formal excellence that made it an ideal vehicle for the kind of representational reflection contained in *The Cherubinic Wanderer*. This is true not only for thematic variety and intensiveness of speculation but also for the very function of this particular verse: the Alexandrine line. It derived from the old French *Roman d'Alexandre* and came into German literature through French classicism, and it became the typical verse for German Baroque poetry and tragedy. It consists of six iambic feet with a strong ceasura in the middle of the third foot:

$$x—x—x—/x—x—x—$$

The Rose

The rose which here on earth is now perceived by me,
Has blossomed thus in God from all eternity. (1:108)

INTRODUCTION

The ultimate foot may be masculine or feminine, providing for twelve or thirteen syllables. Rhymes are often tied to it, but they remain optional, and they are secondary to the structure of the verse. The beat tends to become monotonous. However, especially in the short, laconic epigram, the possibilities of counterbalancing the regularity of the couplet by using the four half-verses with all sorts of highly refined rhetorical arguments are almost infinite. It is thus a poetic receptacle well suited for intellectual and speculative treatment, whether mystical reflection or irony, sardonic or even saucy sagacity using stylistic brilliance for ending with a punchline by means of unexpected twists and turns. Scheffler was a *poeta doctus*, a learned man of letters not given to affective outbursts in poetic writing. He molded the epigram into a perfect solution for the intrinsic problem of any mystical writer: saying the ineffable. He fully exploited the mechanics and function of this particular form to express his speculations in the figures of the paradox, the antithetical anomaly, amplification, intellectual tautologies, and the like.

Any author who uses such an elaborate and stylized form draws his poetic skills from specific models and sources. In Scheffler's case, the context that allowed him to shape the epigrammatic craft into spiritual art is, for the most part, well known. But critics have steadfastly ignored a biblical variation of the epigrammatic tradition that Scheffler, in his preface, mentions by name and that had been used by the desert fathers right through the Middle Ages into the Renaissance: the practice of compiling personal anthologies of biblical verse for contemplative prayer. In the Renaissance, this took a particular form among pietists, who liked to compile seemingly contradictory biblical passages ("paradoxa") that they then used for devout illumination. The most famous author in German-speaking culture using this technique was Sebastian Franck (1499–1542), whose *Paradoxa ducenta octoginta* (1534) belongs most decisively in the tradition from which Jacob Böhme eventually developed some of his basic (dialectic) concepts. As an illustration, I use a more modest collection by a contemporary of Franck, Hans Denck (ca. 1500–1527), who also belongs intellectually in the wider context of Schwenckfeldians. His forty paradoxa (1526), undoubtedly heavily influenced by the writings of John Tauler, contain lines such as these:

a) God wills that all men should be saved. (1 Tm 2:1)
b) Few are chosen. (Mt. 20:16)

13

a) No one has seen God. (Jn 1:18)
b) I have seen the Lord, face to face. (Gn 32:31)[18]

Obviously, the "paradoxa" are not true contradictions but rather serve to instruct and familiarize the reader with basic concepts of faith in a highly condensed form.

As previously mentioned, it was Abraham von Franckenberg who seems to have been the motivating force behind Scheffler's active attempt to write down intellectual insights in the form of short couplets.[19] This was accepted practice in von Franckenberg's circle even though we have little tangible evidence for it; there are, however, two notable exceptions, the aforementioned Daniel Czepko, and the mystic poet Johann Theodor von Tschesch (1595–1649). Whether Scheffler knew the latter personally is unknown. But since von Franckenberg highly esteemed him, it is most likely that Scheffler had read some of his poetry before engaging in the initial writing of *The Cherubinic Wanderer* in the early fifties. More important was Daniel Czepko's already mentioned collection of religious epigrams, *The Monodisticha*, which must have been a major inspiration in terms of both content and style. Jeffrey Sammons cites several examples where couplets show a similarity that speaks for itself:

Monodisticha: Auff Mit Dem Hertzen!

Verachtlich ist der Mensch, der untern Menschen lebt
Und sich nicht uber das, was menschlich ist, erhebt. (1:46)

Lift Your Heart!

Contemptible is the man who lives among men
And does not lift himself beyond that which is human.

The Cherubinic Wanderer: Erheb Dich Uber Dich

Der Mensch der seinen Geist nicht uber sich erhebt/
Der ist nicht wert, dass er im Menschenstande lebt. (2:22)

---

18. Edward J. Furcha, ed. and trans., *Selected Writings of Hans Denck* (Pittsburgh, 1975), 138–39. Franck's collection has, unfortunately, not yet been translated.
19. Gnadinger, "Angelus Silesius," 561.

INTRODUCTION

Lift Yourself above Yourself

The man who does not lift his spirit above itself
He is not worthy of living in the human condition.[20]

It is not just the identical rhyme that attests to more than an elective affinity; Scheffler is heavily indebted to Czepko even though both in style and depth he is undoubtedly superior.

Ever since Benno von Wiese's analysis of antithesis in *The Cherubinic Wanderer*, it has been fashionable to determine two basic types of figures of thought in the couplets.[21] A first one would be the logical reversal of a relation; the second would be a negation, leading to an affirmation of a new entity. An example for the first figure would be:

One is the Beginning and the End of the Other

God is my final end: if I in Him begin,
He takes His being from me and I am lost in Him. (1:276)

An example for the latter:

To God Everything Is Present

No future and no past! What is about to be
Forever was in God perceived essentially. (2:182)

While there is no doubt about the antithetical basis of most of the couplets and verses, there is the danger of reductionism and simplification when one does not look further into the many rhetorical intricacies with which Scheffler tries to reflect the subtlety of his spiritual speculation in the *ductus* of his style and language. The religious reader who tries to transcend the impression of aesthetic achievement will discover many fine figures and shifts, radiating a multiplicity of meanings and facets that are rooted in the Baroque urge to dazzle with a variety of images and at the same time penetrate beyond the sign: content-function of poetic expression into the ineffable.

---

20. Sammons, *Angelus Silesius*, 49; his translations.
21. Benno von Wiese, "Die Antithetik in den Alexandrinern des Angelus Silesius," *Euphorion* XXIX (1929), 503–22; Elisabeth Spörri, *Der Cherubinische Wandersmann als Kunstwerk* (Horgen, 1947), 32; and Sammons, *Angelus Silesius*, 52.

INTRODUCTION

In elegance and flexibility, Scheffler did achieve a degree comparable to the best of the (English) Metaphysical poets. In concluding this introduction of the poetics of *The Cherubinic Wanderer*, let us demonstrate, therefore, some of the skill with which he directed the flow of his verse in figure and rhythm.[22] As pointed out earlier, the basic structure of the couplet in Alexandrine verse is four fairly separable half-verses. This corresponds to a basic balance of two parallel or antithetic statements.

The Spiritual Sowing

God is a husbandman, His seed His only Word,
The ploughshare is His Spirit, my heart the sowing ground. (1:64)

Overlaying such a balance and counterbalance is the juxtaposition of key terms. In the above example they are located at the beginning and the end of the verses, but the antithesis is also carried to the end of the first half-line of each verse and the beginning of the opposing second half-verse. In rhetorical terms, such an interlacing is called chiasmus; the intertwining of thought and speech is perfectly matched. Where necessary, Angelus Silesius resorts to just the opposite stylistic means in order to express something different, as in the following example, where the first half-verse and the fourth half-verse form the link; therefore, half-verses two and three are connected in such a way as to almost eliminate the hiatus at the end of the first full verse:

Creatures Are God's Echo

Nothing is without voice: God everywhere can hear
Arising from creation his praise and echo clear. (1:264)

The poet uses rhetorical tropes and really achieves harmony between the intellectual figure and the actual statement; in the following example the paradox expressed through litotes (circumscription through emphasized hyperbolic opposition) does truly reflect the higher harmony aimed for:

Diversity Is Pleasing

The more we let each voice sound forth with its own tone,
The more diverse will be the chant in unison. (1:268)

---

22. Rhetorical terms are used according to Heinrich Lausberg, *Elemente der literarischen Rhetorik* (München, 1963).

The beginning of each of these verses with the same word introducing an identical syntactical structure (anaphora) is balanced by the two rhyme-words that "literally" sound in harmony! When the mystic's language fails, he turns this shortcoming into an affirmation of his inability by using an accumulation of words articulating the same notion (periphrasis) and coming out of this accumulation of terms (diaeresis) with the concept really sought for:

The Knowing Must Become the Known

In God is nothing known: He is undivided, One,
That which one knows in Him, one must oneself become. (1:285)

The important role played by rhetorical figures and tropes in the mystical verse of *The Cherubinic Wanderer* will be more fully developed in the next section, when the representational character of seventeenth-century poetry is further determined by the mystical context in which this collection is situated.

3. *The Mystical Context*

Every mystical experience and expression takes place in a specific context. Angelus Silesius's conversion has been the cause of apologetic claims and allegations by both Catholics and Protestants—sometimes revealing valuable insights but often obfuscating the beauty of *The Cherubinic Wanderer* by setting Catholic orthodoxy against Lutheran pietism and vice versa. In the extreme instance, there was even an attempt to absolve Scheffler from suspected notions of heresy in connection with Meister Eckhart's views, which had "spilled over" into the Baroque collection.[23] A second, and in our opinion equally detrimental, tendency has been to establish for the truly speculative reflection in almost every poem by Angelus Silesius a string of *loci orthodoxi*—if possible stemming directly from the *Summa Theologica*.[24] Unfortunately, this qualification applies to the most erudite

---

23. Ernst Otto Reichert, *Johannes Scheffler als Streittheologe* . . . , (Gütersloh, 1967), gives an excellent summary of the views of nineteenth-century positivists and virulent Catholic replies in chap. 4 of his study, 33–49.

24. C. Seltmann, *Angelus Silesius und seine Mystik* (Breslau, 1896); an instructive book for students of Catholic dogma with its sources of reference for particular couplets and groupings of central images, but his study as a whole is marred by his obsession with defending the *Cherubinic Wanderer* against all kinds of modern and not-so-modern allegations of nonorthodoxy.

attempt to locate and specify Scheffler's main models. H. Gies's convincing proof of why the Jesuit Sandaeus's compendium *Clavis ero theologia mystica* has to be regarded as the main source for *The Cherubinic Wanderer* is extremely lopsided.[25] Besides stereotyped affirmations of Scheffler's orthodoxy, there is a rather forced attempt to "prove" correspondences by pointing out questionable verbal homologies where loose analogy would be more appropriate. This is all the more regrettable as it is precisely in the rhetorical formation of thought and speech that Scheffler excels, and not in innovation regarding fundamental theology or language, as was the case with the medieval German mystics. Gies is one of the many scholars who, in this particular domain, does not see the proverbial forest for the trees. They forget that, until fairly recently, teaching of the humanities, especially in theology, was done with manuals that were not "original texts" in our sense, but rather digests, compendia, collections, and excerpts that were handed down in a catechism-like format. In the age of Baroque, which was characterized by eclecticism, this instructional technique was, of course, very widely practiced in formal and informal learning.[26] The *Theologia Mystica* of Sandaeus is representative of this; it contains not only a broad range of historical references but also variety in terms of national origin: Latin sources, writings from contemporary Spanish mystics, and so forth. But its main feature is the short and concise excerpt, which lends itself to the type of rhetorical transformation that Scheffler undertook with mystical thought. However, rather than dwell any longer on this question of direct and systematic links and dependencies, let us examine the main qualities and the limitations of *The Cherubinic Wanderer* in the mystical context.

The mystical collection of verse is more homologous to the period in which it was written than might appear at first glance. Modern historians are discovering that the Counter-Reformation was not just a reaction to the rise of Lutheranism and Protestantism; it was also a broad movement inspiring a variety of learned and popular reform movements within the Catholic Church.[27] Probably the most prominent one was the creation and

---

25. *Eine lateinische Quelle zum "Cherubinischen Wandersmann" des Angelus Silesius. Untersuchungen der Beziehungen zwischen der mystischen Dichtung Schefflers und der 'Clavis . . .' des Maximilian Sandaeus* (Breslau, 1929).

26. Cf. Jaime Tarraco, "Angelus Silesius und die spanische Mystik. Die Wirkung spanischer Mystik auf den Cherubinischen Wandersmann," *Görres-Gesellschaft, Spanische Forschungen* I, 1960. 1–150. Informative remarks suffer from the author's fixation on establishing a direct link between Neo-Catholic Spanish mystics and Scheffler.

27. Representative of the older school is Karl Brandi's classic Deutsche *Geschichte im Zeitalter der Reformation und Gegenreformation* (Darmstadt, 1960; 1. Aufl., 1927). For a modern

subsequent spread of the Jesuit Order; we have already seen their important influence in Silesia during Scheffler's spiritual formation. Especially during the time of his conversion, the poet came into contact with St. Ignatius's gift to Western spirituality, *The Spiritual Exercises.* In spite of many voices stressing the importance of the "conversion" character of *The Cherubinic Wanderer*,[28] especially in the first two books, critics have not yet undertaken the task of determining this religious act of Scheffler as the structural principle of the collection. Instead there has been much effort to make thematic, formal, or biographical clusters resemble some rudimentary form fitting into one of the traditional literary genres. *The Spiritual Exercises* (1548), conceived and designed for a directed retreat, has as its ultimate aim the radical change in the "disposition of the mind" of the reader/ practitioner. Ignatius developed with great care and circumspection the gradual transition from acts of contrition to meditative prayer on topics like vices or the nativity and finally the passion and glory of Jesus Christ. "Three Methods of Prayer," preceeding "The Mysteries of the Life of Christ our Lord" (261ff.) describes "The Method" determining the second type of prayer (prefaced by instructions as to physical attitude) as follows (252):

> The Second Method of Prayer is that the person, kneeling or seated, according to the greater disposition he finds himself and as more devotion accompanies him, keeping the eye closed or fixed on one place, without going wandering with them, says FATHER, and is on the consideration of this word as long as he finds meanings, comparisons, relish and consolation in considerations pertaining to such word. And let him do in the same way on each word of the OUR FATHER, or of any other prayer which he wants to say in this way.[29]

Short "Rules" and "Notes" elaborate this prescription. The third method

---

view, cf. Jean Delumeau, *Le peche et la peur. La culpabilite en Occident XIIIe–XVIIIe siecles* (Paris, 1983). One of the qualities of this book is its broad scope; extensive discussion of popular devotion is paralleled with the intellectual historical developments. Cf. note 13 of this introduction.

28. E.g., Alois Haas, "Angelus Silesius. Die Welt—ein wunderschönes Nichts," in *Sermo Mysticus. Studien zu Theologie und Sprache der deutschen Mystik* (Freiburg, Switzerland, 1979), 380ff. (Dokimion 4). Cf. Matthew Fox's *Breakthrough: Meister Eckhart's Creation Spirituality in New Translation* (Garden City, N.Y., 1980).

29. I quote from the edition of David L. Fleming, S.J., *A Literal and Contemporary Reading* (St. Louis, 1978), using the traditional enumeration of sections.

of prayer, which ties this type of contemplative prayer to a breathing exercise and a more profound consideration of the relation between the soul and the Creator, takes on mystical dimensions. It seems obvious that Angelus Silesius's method of poetic reflection and contemplation has more than an elective affinity to St. Ignatius's instruction on contemplative prayer. Direction, terseness, brevity, centeredness, orientation, thematic variety, all fall into place once the reader accepts that the contemplative character of each couplet or poem of *The Cherubinic Wanderer* is a dialectically self-contained capsule meditation and, simultaneously, part of a specific view of the religious matters that constitute the subject for meditation. In this way, the reader can also accept the sequential progress and the arbitrary movement from image to image, sometimes resting for just one couplet, in other instances digressing for half a dozen or more separate reflections on a given notion or icon.[30]

This laconic style is quite distinct from a specific Jesuit form of poetic piety that flourished in Germany at this time and led to at least one other collection of great spirituality and beauty, Friedrich Spee's (1599–1635) posthumously published *Trutzrachtigall* (Holy nightingale) (1649).[31] Angelus Silesius's other poetic collection, *Heilige Seelenlust* (The holy joy of the soul) published with *The Cherubinic Wanderer*, stands in this tradition; its bucolic genre images, however, which reflect the Baroque's enthrallment with shepherd life transformed into religious imagery, are not as directly accessible to a modern reader as the epigrammatic couplets. Since this collection is available only in German, one typical example might demonstrate how a similar disposition could find a quite different poetic expression in so-called seraphic verse, the emotional as opposed to the more abstract and reflective "cherubinic." Rhymes have been abandoned in the translation, but images are rendered as literally as possible in order to show the contrast:

Rose-Wounds
The Soul longs to be a little Bee on Jesus' Wounds

1

Green twig, you noble scion,
You blossom rich in honey,

---

30. Cf. Louise Gnädinger's observation of this second point in her article on Scheffler (see note 4), 562.
31. Another master of Jesuit devotional poetry in the Neolatin tradition was Jacob Balde (1604–1648).

INTRODUCTION

You paradise reopened,
Grant me this supplication:
Let my soul be a little bee
Dwelling on your rose-wounds.

2

I long dearly for their juice,
I seek them with great pains,
For they grant power and strength
For tired hearts;
So let me be a little bee
Dwelling on your rose-wounds.

3

Their exquisite fragrance
Is a fragrance giving life.
It kills the poison, obliterates the curse,
It elevates the spirit;
For this let me be a little bee
Dwelling on your rose-wounds.

4

My heart, my mouth—
They kiss them a thousand times.
Let me rejoice at all hours
In your honey juice;
Let my soul be a little bee
Dwelling on your rose-wounds.

5

O sweet honey-dew!
How lovely you are in my soul,
How good to be on this meadow
And rest in such a flower-cove.
Let me always be a little bee
Dwelling on your rose-wounds.

6

Take my mind, my spirit and my sense;
Take body, soul

And all that I possess;
That I forever be a little bee
Dwelling on the wounds of Lord Jesus Christ.[32]

The reader will also recognize from certain images that church songs and hymns left their trace in both *The Cherubinic Wanderer* and *The Holy Joy of the Soul*.

Besides knowing the most popular devotional book of that time, *The Imitation of Christ*, Scheffler knew other writings of the Upper Rhenish mystical movement, above all those by Jan van Ruusbroec. And he uses images and reflective premises from another classic, dating back to the late fourteenth century and reissued by Martin Luther in 1516/1518: *The Theologia Germanica* of the anonymous Frankfurter.[33] An outgrowth of a spiritual movement, "the friends of God," this very sober treatise represents a symbiosis of mainstream Christian mysticism, combining Dionysius the Aeropagite with a thorough knowledge of Tauler and other medieval figures and their works. It is practically oriented as a handbook for Christian spirituality, not abundant in images, but rich in plain explanation of the heritage of medieval German mysticism. Whether it is the controversial "ground of being" of Meister Eckhart (chapter 33), where God reveals himself as the Creator in the created, the "spark of the soul," and the negative formulation of the Godhead as the ultimate "Nothing," who is above and beyond all names, or the notion of divinization (chapter 14)—all is presented in a straight and forthright manner. Some of these notions will be illustrated further in the concluding section of this Introduction. What should be stressed here, however, are two key perspectives that Scheffler undoubtedly absorbed from either this work or the sermons by Tauler: the distinction between the interior and the exterior eye, and the disposition of indifference for proper conversion to mystical union. The two ways to see the creation and the Creator are intimately tied to the concept of the inner eye as being the uncorrupted, Adamic view given to man by God. Transformation of the outer, worldly, and corrupted way of seeing things is one of the main themes in *The Cherubinic Wanderer*. "Gelassenheit" (dy-

---

32. Cf. text and interpretation by Louise Gnädinger in Martin Bircher and Alois Haas, eds. *Deutsche Barocklyrik, Gedichtinterpretationen von Spee bis Haller* (Bern, 1973), 97–133.

33. Cf. the edition translated and introduced by Bengt Hoffmann in The Classics of Western Spirituality (New York/Ramsey/Toronto, 1980). There is a substantial introduction to a German edition published the same year (Einsiedeln: Johannes Verlag) by Alois Haas. The enumeration of chapters in Hoffmann's edition differs from the above and that in other German editions.

namic indifference/inner serenity and peace/detachment/equanimity) is a condition entered into after long and complete subjugation of the individual's will to the will of God (chapter 25). It is also one of the key notions of Ignatian spirituality. In negative terms, one has to point out that the *German Theology* does maintain, unlike the German mystics and, probably, Angelus Silesius, the traditional three-step model of the mystical ways of purgation, illumination, and union (chapter 24) as opposed to the conviction of the latter of entering into union by way of a breakthrough with the help of *scientia divina*, godly inspiration.[34]

As stated in the biographical sketch, Scheffler became very reticent after his conversion about admitting the pietistic roots of his spirituality because of his obsessive concern with Catholic orthodoxy. At the same time, we know about his interest in medieval mystics and his deep friendship with Abraham von Franckenberg, who had an intimate relationship with the most influential thinker of that movement, Jakob Böhme (1575–1624). But before the Silesian shoemaker's basic thoughts are sketched, a few words should be addressed to how the spiritualist movement became the carrier of pietism outside both Lutheran and Catholic mainstream religion. Since hardly any texts by the more famous proponents of that pietism are available in English, a brief outline shall suffice.[35]

Caspar Schwenckfeld (1489–1561), a Silesian who became the main inspiration for a variety of groups and sects, developed concepts of rebirth, indifference, and regeneration in the context of a noninstitutional church, leading to his persecution by both Catholics and Lutherans.[36] But his writings and ideas survived and led to the creation of several communities and more informal groups such as that of Abraham von Franckenberg in the seventeenth century. Another powerful writer was Valentin Weisel (1553–1588), in addition to the already mentioned Sebastian Franck. In spite of persecution, particularly of anabaptists and enthusiasts, this spirituality lasted through the centuries following the Reformation, and one of the regions where it remained a pervasive movement was Silesia. Angelus Silesius's experience with censorship was shared, in a more severe form, by

---

34. Cf. Alois Haas, "Meister Eckharts geistliches Predigtprogramm," in *Ereiburger Zeitschrift für Philosophie und Theologie* 27, 1/2 (1982), 195 and *passim*.

35. Exceptions to the rule are anthologies, like volume 25 of *The Library of Christian Classics, Spiritual and Anabaptist Writers*, ed. by George Huntston Williams et al. (Philadelphia, 1957). On pp. 285–293 there is the informative "Bibliography of Material in English Translation written by Representatives of the Radical Reformation (1524–1575)." But translation of major treatises remains a desideratum.

36. Cf. Edward J. Furcha, *Schwenckfeld's Concept of the New Man: A Study in the Anthropology of C.v.S. as set forth in his Major Theological Writings* (Pennsburg, 1970); 41f., 46ff., 53ff.

INTRODUCTION

Jakob Böhme. Despite being forced to change his line of business and his residence, and being forbidden to publish by the Lutheran pastor of his native town of Görlitz, Böhme managed to compose massive volumes of profound mysticism, which were first circulated by hand and later published and widely distributed. His nonacademic erudition was based mainly on oral tradition; this accounts for the complexity and the originality of his writing, but also for some of its obscurantist features and long-windedness. Some key notions have found their way directly into *The Cherubinic Wanderer*. Böhme's understanding of God as the great Nothing stems from a progressive series of three principles—the good, the evil, and the materialistic—being reflected in the human soul. His gnostic model is of little importance in this context, but his concept of language undoubtedly influenced Scheffler. The *lingua adamica* or natural language was the state of human communication before the fall and original sin, and the way back to rediscovering God's nature and His creation was elaborately set out in the posthumously printed *De Signatura Rerum* (The signification of all things). Rebirth through immersion in adamic language remained a permanent idea in his writing, even in a lucid and tightly structured devotional book like *The Way to Christ* (the only large work published during his lifetime).[37]

One can only guess as to which extant liturgical forms in the vernacular, church hymns, and other forms of popular devotion shaped *The Cherubinic Wanderer*. But their influence was strong and shines through, for example, in the third book of the collection in many couplets on the nativity or the feasts of patron saints. We can also deduce from the appearance of some of the verses in the folklore of later times that their popularity was derived, in part, from the fact that tradition was a godparent in the creation of the work.

In conclusion, then, it should be evident that *The Cherubinic Wanderer* is a receptacle for many streams of the Christian mystical tradition, coined in a well-polished and most appropriate poetic currency, the versatile epigram. As its angelic name suggests, it is a speculative collection of pious reflections containing the positive and negative aspects of such eclecticism: an incredibly wide range of themes, concepts, and images, but no systematic or creative structure except for an Ignatian forcefulness of perspective toward conversion.[38] Its joy and exuberance in spiritual contemplation, its

---

37. Trans. and intro. by Peter Erb (New York/Ramsey/Toronto, 1978; The Classics of Western Spirituality).

38. Something comparable in another form of spirituality of that age can be found in

24

delight in ever-new formulations of traditional and established thoughts and figures as a heuristic way to seek access to God, and its representational abundance make it truly a child of its age, the Baroque, and of the great spiritual tradition enabling its creation.

4. Spiritual Notions

While there is no formal structure to the six books of *The Cherubinic Wanderer*, they do vary with regard to themes. Books 1 and 2 abound in speculative theology on the great themes of God, nothing, divinization, time/eternity, angels, I/self-will/detachment, man as created creation, and rebirth. The third book contains a kind of corrective to the many concepts of negative theology in that there is a multitude of christological and bridal-mystical notions and also many epigrams on patron saints and the theme of the nativity of Jesus. Books 4 and 5 return to a more speculative train of thought, while in book 6 there are many apologetic verses, together with a sizable number of popular themes, often written in the *genus humile* style. This book also contains the recognizable influence of emblems, pictorially ornamented epigrams that were very popular in the Renaissance and the Baroque.

Clusters of images and key concepts are loosely connected through association, sometimes lingering for an extended series of configurations, more often hurrying on to new and ever more sophisticated figures of cherubinic speculation by way of analogy, paradox, and saying the opposite. Saying the ineffable is closely related to Catholic teaching on the highest order of angels, the Seraphim and Cherubim. While a more emotional nature is attributed to Seraphim, Cherubim were traditionally directly associated with the *scientia indita*, an innate knowledge of connatural insights into the nature of God—not verbalized, but bestowed on them from the beginning. There is rich evidence in the New Testament (e.g. Mt 18:10) of the angelic tradition that turned into extensive speculation on the nature of angels throughout the Middle Ages. Angelus Silesius did not add to this knowledge, but made derivative use of the intrinsic theological dilemma of angelic articulation: to praise God not through manifestations of earthly

---

the sermons of Abraham a Sancta Clara (1644–1709), court preacher in Vienna, whose immense popularity and down-to-earth language also reflect an incredibly wide eclectic knowledge of theological traditions and sources. Cf. his *Grammatica Religiosa* (Salzburg, 1699) where the Bible, St. Thomas, and St. Bernard of Clairvaux speak side-by-side with proverbs and puns.

realities but rather through signification. This is the main reason for the high level of abstraction characterizing many of his verses, and also the relatively scarce use of biblical paraphrase.

As stated above, *The Cherubinic Wanderer* is primarily a book of contemplative prayer exercising the soul in Ignatian conversion to become aware of *de signatura rerum* in theological terms; the essence of things and truths is reached through poetic meditation.[39] A truly thematic couplet near the beginning of *The Cherubinic Wanderer* exemplifies both the substance and the dilemma of this spiritual exercise:

One Cannot Grasp God

God is the purest naught, untouched by time and space.
The more you reach for Him, the more He will escape. (1:25)

Angelus Silesius later comments as follows:

The Silent Prayer

God far exceeds all words that we can here express
In silence he is heard, in silence worshiped best. (1:240)

Both couplets reverberate with one of German medieval mysticism's most central notions: "The more one seeks you, the less one finds you. You should so seek him that you find him nowhere. If you do not seek him, then you will find him."[40]

A configuration of this rhetorically condensed thought can be recognized in the searching phrase of Jakob Böhme:

The more reason sinks into absurd humility before God, and the more unworthy it holds itself [to be] before God, [so much] more it dies to its own desire; and [so much] more it is pierced through by God's

---

39. An excellent survey, Louis L. Martz's *The Poetry of Meditation: A Study in English Religious Literature of the 17th Century* (New Haven and London, 1962, 2nd ed.), discusses the classical treatises and their application in depth (I:1,1, and I:3,4).

40. Sermon 15 on Lk 19:20. Quoted from *Meister Eckhart: The Essential Sermons, Commentaries, Treatises, and Defense*, trans. and intro. by Edmund Colledge and Bernard McGinn (New York/Ramsey/Toronto, 1981; The Classics of Western Spirituality), 192. For a list of *loci classici* from the New Testament and the church fathers, see Seltmann, 94ff.

Spirit, who brings it to the highest knowledge, so that it may see the great wonders of God.[41]

Compare this with the plain admonition of *The Imitation of Christ:*

My son, hear My words. They are of surpassing sweetness, and exceed all learning of the philosophers and wise men of this world. My words are spirit and life, not to be weighed by man's understanding. They are not to be quoted for vain pleasure, but are to be heard in silence.[42]

In the fourth book, Angelus Silesius combines this mystical notion with an almost complete catalog of scholastic categories of the essence of God, again thematizing ineffability:

The Unknowable God

One knows not what God is. Not spirit and not light,
Not one, truth, unity, not what we call divine.
Not reason and not wisdom, not goodness, love or will,
No thing, no nothing either, not being or concern.
He is what I or you, or any other creature
Has never come to know before we were created. (4:21)

Many key notions filtered through to Angelus Silesius in a specific book, *Maximil, Sandaei S.J. pro Theologia mystica clavis* (Cologne, 1640), a "key" to mystical theology; in individual chapters on *deificatio, deiformitas, unio,*" and so forth, pertinent passages are listed in lexicon form. Hildegardis Gies has found some astounding homologies of Baroque excerpts, Scheffler's versifications, and writings from the church fathers. Consider the following link concerning divinization:

We Become What We Love (From Augustine)

Man, you shall be transformed into that which you love:
Earth, if you love the earth; God, if you love your God. (5:200)

---

41. For Böhme, see endnote 37, 123 (4, 36).
42. *The Imitation of Christ* is quoted from the Penguin translation of Leo Sherley-Price (Harmondsworth, 1978), 93 (III:3).

The *clavis* contains the following passage:

Augustinus autem tractatu II. in epistolam Joan. ita ratiocinatur: Quemadmodum, qui terram diligit, terra erit: sic qui Deum, erit Deus. (p. 434)
(St. Augustine in his treatise on St. John's letter reasons as follows: Similarly, whoever loves the world, will be world, and likewise whoever loves God, will be God.)[43]

The manner of achieving this transformation has been the unending appeal of the medieval mystical tradition of abnegating one's own will and letting the self-will be totally immersed in the Lord. The *Theologia Germanica* is almost literally quoted in

Der Ichheit Tod Stärkt In Dir Gott

So viel mein Ich in mir verschmachtet und abnimmt,
So viel des Herren Ich dafür zu Kräften kommt. (5:126)

The more Mine and I, that is to say I-attachment and
selfishness, recede, the more God's I, that is God
Himself, increases in me. (chap. 24)[44]

In his attempt to grasp the incomprehensible, Angelus Silesius expresses in hyperbolic terms his desire to transcend even angelic cognition:

One Must Go beyond Thought

What Cherubim may know will never bring me peace,
Outstrip I must all thought, the highest goal to reach. (1:284)

In the canon of mystical imagery of the gap between perception, thought, and experience; the abyss; and the sun have held a prominent position, partly because of their roots in the Psalms, but also because of the multiplicity of meanings and reflections that they could encompass. And they could, of course, be coupled with their opposites in order to transcend the barriers of literal language, of denotation and connotation.

That Scheffler should use images of night from St. John of the Cross is no surprise:

---

43. See Gies, endnote 25, 84.
44. *Theologia Germanica*, see endnote 33, 79.

INTRODUCTION

The Blessed Silence of the Night

If your soul can be still as night to the created,
God becomes man in you, retrieves what's violated. (3:8)

Transitus animae ad unionem divinam . . . nox appelatur
accomodate.
(The transition of the soul into divine union is appropriately called
night.)[45]

The sun is praised in many reflections and functions. The following image
of its essence can be found in exegetical abundance in practically all mystical texts, two particularly shining examples of which are John Tauler's
Sermon X for the 5th Saturday of Lent on John 8:12 "I am the light of the
world," and the twenty-fourth chapter of the *Theologia Germanica*, where
the sun, when asked "Why do you shine?" answers: "I have to shine and
can do nothing else. It is my nature. It is in me to shine."[46]

I Must Be the Sun

Myself I must be sun, whose rays must paint the sea,
The vast and unhued ocean of all divinity. (1:115)

From the work of Tauler, one of the boldest synesthetic clusters of images
has found its way through the *clavis* into Baroque verse:

One Abyss Calls the Other

The abyss that is my soul invokes unceasingly
The abyss that is my God. Which may the deeper be? (1:68)

Abyssus tenebrarum omnium suarum . . . divinae invocit caliginis
abyssum.
(One's abyss of all darkness invokes the abyss of dark divinity.)

And to quote once more the heavy and grasping version of this image in
Jakob Böhme's vision:

---

45. See Gies, 36.
46. *Spiritual Conferences by Johann Tauler*, trans. and ed. Eric Colledge and Sister M.
Jane, O.P. (Rockford, Ill., 1978), 57–63., *Theologia Germanica*, 95.

Since the abyss, as God, is an eternal speaking, a breathing out of Himself, so also the abyss is spoken into resigned life. The abyss' breathing speaks through the static ground life. Life has arisen out of divine breathing and is a likeness of the divine breathing.[47]

One may also notice how similar Angelus Silesius and Böhme are in their ability to shift from image to image trying to encompass the full range of penetrating expression. However, Scheffler is not averse to becoming very terse, lifting Latin quotations straight into the Alexandrine, as the following image of the abyss demonstrates:

> *Summa Theologica:* In inferno non est vera aeternitas, sed magis tempus.

In Hell There Is No Eternity

> Reflect on this with care: God is eternity;
> With the devil in hell, eternal time will be.[48] (5:74)

Man, creation, and rebirth as presented in *The Cherubinic Wanderer* have often been misunderstood in later times as leaning heavily toward pantheistic notions. But even Scheffler's highly condensed pronouncements on incarnation represent dazzling rhetorical sophistication, rather than leaving the realm of Christian theology. Three subthemes of this question may serve as illustrations of the problem: Mary, alchemy, and the use of Eckhart's "spark of the soul."

The Spiritual Virgin

> The Virgin I must be and bring God forth from me,
> Should ever I be granted divine felicity. (1:23)

Often, such verses—other examples of this theme of speculation are 3:28 and 4:16—have caused misconceptions because of incomplete knowledge of Catholic devotional tradition. In this particular instance, the Mariological devotion, incarnation, and the role of grace are so densely expressed that they are hardly recognizable in a first reading. If one accepts, however,

---

47. Gies, 100; Böhme, 209 (7, 21).
48. von Balthasar, 98 (*Summa Theologica* I:103 c et ad 2).

that this is a collection of verse for meditative prayer, one can retrace the composition of mystical imagery quite easily; the title is a truly exegetical pointer on how to combine and venture forth into this aspect of Christian salvation.

Some of the alchemistic images are accessible even today and do not need a commentary:

The Tincture

The Holy Spirit smelts, the Father does consume,
The Son the tincture is, which gilds and does transmute. (1:246)

Here the alchemistic process is overlain with the image of the interaction of the Holy Trinity. However, in other couplets, spiritualist imagery must leave the reader puzzled by its enigmatic Baroque chemistry!

Nature Is Threefold

The Godhead is triune, as every plant reveals;
Sulphur, salt, mercury are all in one concealed. (1:257)

There is a hierarchy guiding these elements, which are used in the spiritualist alchemistic tradition of "designation of all things" according to Jakob Böhme. "Sulphur as the source begets mercury, the divider, from which two salts arise. All three reflect the trinity in man."[49] This hierarchy is also apparent in references to God and the universe (the elements correspond to specific planets)—in fact, even in the "characteristics (*Eigenschaften*) of things and the "tempermentum (*sic*) of every person. The mystical model is thus again all-encompassing although transmitted in the modest form of a poetic couplet.

Probably the best-known innovative notion stemming from medieval German mysticism is "the spark of the soul" (*scintilla*)—but it is also one of the least understood. This, in turn, is a function of its complexity as a concept of the dynamic interaction between God and man. It is not a pantheistic euphemism for some vague mystical link but an icon of the most intimate, innermost center of the soul where God can be experienced.[50] No

---

49. Böhme, intro. by Peter Erb, 24.
50. Alois Haas, *Meister Eckhart als normative Gestalt geistlichen Lebens* (Einsiedeln, 1979), 48ff. See also *Horst Althaus: Johann Schefflers "Cherubinischer Wandersmann": Mystik und Dichtung* (Giessen, 1956), 22, 32 and *passim*.

wonder that even the knowledgeable mystic seeks unendingly for fitting metaphors. Angelus Silesius makes the most of the verses he uses when grouping cosmic images, broken by intellectual figures manifesting the relation between Creator and created in the following sequence of couplets:

The Brook Becomes the Sea

Here I still flow in God, as does a brook in Time,
There, I shall be the sea of beatitude divine. (4:135)

The Ray Becomes the Sun

My spirit once in God will eternal bliss become;
Just as the sun's own ray is sun within the sun. (4:136)

The Spark in The Fire

Who is it who can tell the spark within the fire?
And who, once within God, can perceive what I am? (4:137)

A firework of rhetorical tropes sparkles from the structural axis of a whole as compared with its part. Elements (fire, water), dimensions (time, eternity), and theological notions (God, bliss) flow into two rhetorical questions thematizing the "spark of the soul," but in mystical, not poetic, reflection on the essence of being.

Naturally, many more themes are contemplated in *The Cherubinic Wanderer*. Above all, images of bridal union, as taken from the writings of Jan van Ruusbroec and others, would have to be generalized in a thorough study of Scheffler's key notions and their origins. But, as Gottfried Arnold (1666–1714), a conciliatory Lutheran pietist who published the collection and thus made it common heritage to both confessions, said, the book is written for and to be used by "a simple yet wise lover of divine mysteries for whom I wish the same spirit of truth which moved the creator of these verses."[51]

---

51. Quoted from Gerhard Desczyk's selection (East-Berlin, 1956), 138.

Or as Angelus Silesius says in his inimitable way in the last couplet of his work:

Conclusion

Friend, let this be enough; if you wish more to read
Go and become yourself the writ and that which is. (6:263)

A Word about the
Textual Notes

The notes, mainly references to various sources, demonstrate the eclectic use of sources by Angelus Silesius. By far the most important source is Maximilian Sandaei, *Pro Theologia mystica clavis* (Cologne, 1640; a reprint appeared 1963 in the *Editions de la Bibliothèque S.J.*, [Heverlee-Louvain, 1963]). The structure of the work consists of an alphabetical list of key concepts and notions of Christian mysticism with numerous references. Two works, compilations of mystical "classics," both of which Scheffler possessed in his library, were particularly used by him: Ludovici Blosii, *Opera*, I (Augsburg, 1626); and Henrici Harpii, *Theologia mystica* (Cologne, 1556). When passages are quoted in the notes, the page number refers to the *Clavis;* a further reference is given to Hildeburgis Gies's monograph on Scheffler's main source (Breslau, 1929) where applicable. Gies consulted Scheffler's copy of the *Clavis;* which contains numerous handwritten additions, underlined passages, etc. Wherever she mentions them, her reference was included. The illustrating examples were chosen according to thematic importance and textual congruences still visible in translation.

Angelus Silesius provided only a handful of biblical references in his edition. Additional references were given where he quotes, paraphrases, or alludes to images from the Old and New Testament.

No specific notes have been made for most couplets referring to the three angelic orders: the Thrones, the Seraphim, and the Cherubim. Angelus Silesius views them traditionally. The nine ranks of angels are subdivided into three hierarchies of three (ternars). He wants the reader to imitate the specific tasks of the highest hierarchy. Like the Cherubim (= spreaders of wisdom), he should knowingly contemplate God; like the Seraphim (= the enflamers), he should love God; and like the Thrones (= the servers), he should submit to the reign of God. Poems 3:165, 4:108, and 5:215 praise these functions; 2:184 stands for the biblical reference to the main reason for the existence of angels (cf. Mt 18:10): that they enjoy the sight of the Godhead.

Couplets used as illustrations in the Introduction are referred to in the notes simply by section (2. The Epigrammatic Tradition; 4. Spiritual Notions).

Book One

Purity of Spirit Will Endure

Pure as the finest gold, hard as the granite stone,
Wholly as crystal clear your spirit must become. (1)

What God Is, You Must Be

Should I my final goal and primal source[1] discover,
I must myself in God and God in me recover
Becoming what He is: a shine within His shine,
A word within His Word, by God be made divine. (6)

One Must Go beyond God

Where is my dwelling place? Where I can never stand.
Where is my final goal, toward which I should ascend?
It is beyond all place. What should my quest then be?
I must, transcending God, into a desert flee. (7)

God in Me and I in Him

God is the fire in me and I in Him the shine;
Are we not with each other most inwardly entwined? (11)

Beyond Divinity

What men have said of God, not yet suffices me,
My life and light is One beyond divinity. (15)

Love Forces God

If it was not God's wish to raise me above God
I should compel him thus, by force of sheerest love. (16)

A Christian Is God's Son

I also am God's Son, I'm sitting at His right,[2]
His Spirit, Flesh, and Blood, He can there recognize. (17)

---

1. The *causa prima*, the first and ultimate (cf. 3:174) goal, is a central scholastic concept of God.

2. The image of Christ sitting at the right hand of God the Father appears twice in important liturgical texts of the daily mass: in the "Gloria" and in the "Apostolic Creed."

ANGELUS SILESIUS

I Do as God Does

God loves me above all; if I love Him the same,
I give Him just as much as I receive from Him. (18)

Beatitude Depends on You

O Man, beatitude is placed within your hands,
If only you submit, and freely give consent. (20)

The Spiritual Virgin

The Virgin I must be and bring God forth from me,[3]
Should ever I be granted divine felicity. (23)

To Be Nothing and Want Nothing

O Man, as long as you exist, know, have, and cherish,
You have not been delivered, believe me, of your burden. (24)

One Cannot Grasp God[4]

God is the purest naught, untouched by time and space
The more you reach for Him, the more He will escape. (25)

The Secret Death

Death is a blessed thing;[5] if it be vigorous,
The life that springs from it will be more glorious. (26)

There Is No Death

I don't believe in death; if every hour I die,
I then shall have each time discovered a better life. (30)

---

3. The concept of God being thus born in man was developed already by the early church fathers. Cf. introduction, section 4.
4. Cf. Introduction, section 4.
5. Cf. Rom 6:8ff.

BOOK ONE

Nothing Lives without Dying

If He should live in you, God first Himself must die,
How would you, without death, inherit His own life?[6] (33)

Death Is the Best Thing[7]

Because through death alone we become liberated,
I say it is the best of all the things created. (35)

No Death Is without Life

I say that nothing dies; just that life eternal
Is given us through death, even the death infernal. (36)

Anxiety Comes from You

It is but you alone that moves and is the wheel,[8]
Running all by itself and never standing still. (37)

One Can Love without Knowing

I love one single thing, it is to me unknown;
And since I know it not, I chose it for my own. (43)

The Blessed No-Thing

I am a blessed thing, could I a no-thing be,
Stranger to all that is, for nobody to see. (46)

Time's Like Eternity

Time's like eternity, eternity like time,
Unless you do yourself between them draw a line. (47)

---

6. Cf. 1 Cor 15:21ff.
7. A clear and concise example for a Christian understanding of death as opposed to the stoic concept held by secular humanists.
8. The wheels of fortune and of history have an old medieval emblematic tradition. In the seventeenth century, the *perpetuum mobile* in the form of a wheel was a much-discussed image.

Body, Soul, and Godhead

The soul a crystal is, the Godhead is her shine;
The body you inhabit hides both as in a shrine. (60)

The Spiritual Sowing[9]

God is a husbandman, His seed His only Word,
The ploughshare is His Spirit, my heart the sowing ground. (64)

One Abyss Calls the Other

The abyss that is my soul invokes unceasingly
The abyss that is my God.[10] Which may the deeper be? (68)

Milk and Wine Give Strength

Humanity is milk, wine the divinity,
If you drink milk and wine, you'll greatly strengthened be. (69)

One Must Be Essence

To love is difficult, for loving's not enough.
Like God we must ourselves become that very love. (71)

How One Sees God

God dwells in light supreme, no path can give access;
Yourself must be that light, if you would there progress. (72)

Return to the Source

The spirit which God breathed when He had made me first,
In essence must return and stand in Him immersed. (74)

---

9. Cf. Introduction, section 2.

10. Cf. Ps 42:8. Scheffler made the following entry into his copy of Sandaeus's *Clavis* under the heading "solitudo" (Gies, 100): "Abyssus tenebrarum omnium suarum . . . divinae invocet caliginis abyssum. Thaul., p. 668 . . . " (The abyss of all the shadows calls on the abyss of divine darkness . . .). This is indeed a key notion of the medieval mystic John Tauler (1300–1361). Cf. also Introduction, section 4.

What You Crave Becomes Your Idol

Crave nothing short of God; I say it clear and strong.
How holy you may be, your idol it will become. (75)

Everything Rests in Its Own Element

The bird flies in the air, the stone rests on the land,
The fish lives in the water, my spirit in God's hand. (80)

God Blossoms in His Branches

If you are born of God, then in you God will green;
His godhead is your sap, your beauty is in Him. (81)

The Godhead Brings Forth Growth

The Godhead is my sap; what in me greens and flowers
It is the Holy Ghost who all the growth empowers. (90)

Totally Divinized

Who is as he were naught and never had been aught,
He, O Beatitude, has wholly become God. (92)

One Sustains the Other

God shelters me as much as I do shelter Him;
His Being I sustain, sustained I am therein. (100)

Christ

Oh, what a marvel! Christ is both Shepherd and Lamb,
When God within my soul today is born a man. (101)

Spiritual Alchemy

Myself I am the metal, spirit the furnace fires,
Messiah[11] is the dye that body and soul inspires. (103)

---

11. The idea of Messiah as man reborn in God is of cabbalistic origin. Scheffler very likely knew about this in connection with alchemy through his friend Abraham v. Franckenberg.

The Same

As soon as I myself in God transmuted be,
Then God impresses me with His own effigy.[12] (104)

The Rose

The rose which here on earth is now perceived by me,
Has blossomed thus in God from all eternity.[13] (108)

The Creatures

If creatures do subsist in God's eternal Son
How can they perish then, or ever naught become? (109)

The Godhead Is a Naught

The tender Godhead is a naught and more than naught;
Who nothing sees in all, believe me, he sees God. (111)

The Sun Is Sufficient

To whom the sun does shine, he should not ever peer,
If elsewhere might the moon and other stars appear. (114)

I Must Be Sun[14]

Myself I must be sun, whose rays must paint the sea,
The vast and unhued ocean of all divinity. (115)

Dew

Dew does the field revive; should it my heart elate,
It must from Jesus' heart itself originate. (116)

---

12. V. Franckenberg's main mentor, Jakob Böhme, made this image of "impressing" the basic mode of mystical-theosophic understanding. One of his main works bears the title *De signatura rerum* (On the referential impression of all things). It is based on the understanding that God impresses his essence into man as soon as he opens himself to divinization.

13. Added to the German text is the note "idealiter," i.e., Scheffler very consciously gave a poetic image for the (Neoplatonic) notion of the archetypal pre-existence of all things.

14. Cf. Introduction, section 4.

BOOK ONE

Through Humanity to God

If you would like to catch dew of divinity,
Unwaveringly adhere to its humanity. (121)

God Laments for His Bride

The turtledove[15] bewails that she has lost her mate,
And so does God that you should choose death in His stead. (123)

You Must Be Newly Born

God has become incarnate; be you not divinized,
You do revile His birth and mock His sacrifice. (124)

Paradise in the Midst of Agony

O Man, cleave close to God and mean but Him alone,
Then agony and toil a paradise become. (131)

It Sustains and Is Sustained

The Word that you and me and everything sustains,[16]
Is in its turn by me sustained and contained. (139)

The Greater the Submission, the Greater the Love

And why is it that God more loves the Seraphim
Than He does love a gnat: See, he submits to Him. (142)

In You Is What You Choose

Hear, Heaven is in you, as is the pain of hell:
You shall have everywhere that which you choose and will. (145)

---

15. This bird, emblematic for love (cf. Sg 2:12 and 14), was famous in classical and medieval bestiaries for the monogamous loyalty referred to in this couplet.
16. Cf. Jn 1:1–3.

The Symbol of the Trinity

Mind, Spirit, and the Word, they teach you clear and free,
That you may apprehend how God is One, yet Three. (148)

Eternal Wisdom

Eternal wisdom[17] goes where all her children dwell.
But why? How marvelous! A child she is as well. (165)

Christ Is Everything

Oh, wondrous mystery! Christ is the truth and Word,
Light, life, food, drink, and path, the ending of my search. (168)

Fundamentally All Are One

One speaks of time and place, present, eternity.
But what are time and place, present, eternity? (177)

The Fault Is Yours

If looking at the sun you be deprived of sight,
Your eyes are then at fault and not the dazzling light. (178)

Eternal Wisdom's House

Eternal Wisdom builds:[18] I shall become the palace,
If she has found in me and I in her all solace. (186)

To Me It's All the Same[19]

I wonder what to do! To me it's all the same:
Place, no-place, eternity, night, day, and joy and pain. (190)

---

17. Jakob Böhme (cf. note to 1:104) also developed an extensive doctrine of divine wisdom ("Sophienlehre"), clothed in a multitude of intertwined images.

18. Cf. Prv 9:1.

19. In Sandaeus's *Clavis*, a classical definition of this state of mind is given (Gies, 29/30; according to Harphius, lib. 2, *Theologia Mystica*, I, *cap.* 12): "Supremus gradus resignationis voluntatis in placatissimam voluntatem Dei, est, quod . . . cito et perfecto Divinam voluntatem sequatur in omnibus, quae sibi venire possunt in tempore, vel in aeternitate . . . " (The highest degree of giving up one's own will and reconciling it with the will of God consists in following swiftly and fully the divine will in everything which can occur in time and eternity . . .).

BOOK ONE

The Creature Is Grounded in God

The creature is to God closer than to itself;
Were it destroyed it would with Him and in Him dwell. (193)

Light Consists of Fire

Light imparts strength to all: Yet were God not the fire,
Though He lives in pure light, He would Himself expire. (195)

God Makes Perfection

He surely lacks belief in God's omnipotence,
Denying me perfection, desired by providence. (197)

The Word Resembles the Fire

Fire incites all things and yet unmoved remains,
Like the Eternal Word, that moves, heaves, generates. (198)

God Is beyond Creatures[20]

Go where you cannot go; see where you cannot see;
Hear where there is no sound, you are where God does speak. (199)

The High Honor

See, how God honors me! Leaping from His high throne,[21]
He places me upon it, in His beloved Son. (202)

---

20. A classical topos, the apophatic mystical approach in which the impossibility of positively comprehending God is thematized. Scheffler's main source, Sandaeus's *Clavis* (196/97; Gies, 46/7), refers here to the classical treatise on the subject in the Western tradition, *Dionysius the Areopagite ad Timotheum* "An elevatio mystica sit, et qualis sit consurrectio et transcensio" (Whether spiritual elevation is mystical, and of what kind consurrection and transcencion are). "Relinque sensus et sensibilia exercitia et etiam intellectuales operationes et omnia sensibilia et intelligibilia et omnia existentia et non existentia. . . . Et sicut est tibi possibile, consurge ignote et supersubstantialiter ad initionem Dei, quae est super omnem substantiam et cognitionem" (Abandon the senses, the active sensibilies and processes of cognition, leave behind you any sensual or intellectual state, all that is and that is not, and thus elevate yourself as much as possible, to that which is unknown and beyond reality into the origin of God which is beyond any substance and comprehension). The *Theologia Germanica* of the "Franckforter," written around 1370, quotes the same passage in the same context (cf. Bengt Hoffman's translation, chapter 8, 68/9, of the *Classics of Western Spirituality series*, 1980).
21. Cf. Wis 18:15.

The Sweetest Revelry

Oh, sweetest revelry! God has become my wine,
Meat, table, serving man, my music when I dine.[22] (207)

The Awesome Difference

The Whore of Babylon drinks blood and thus drinks death;[23]
I do drink blood and God. Oh, awesome difference! (209)

The More Surrendered, the More Divine

The saints are just as drunk[24] with God's divinity,
As they can lose themselves and be immersed in Him. (210)

I, like God, God, like Me

God is that which He is; I am that which I am;
And if you know one well, you know both me and Him. (212)

The Divine Mode of Seeing

If in your neighbor you but God and Christ will see,
Then you see with the light born from divinity. (218)

Faith

Faith, small as mustard seed,[25] plants mountains in the sea:
Reflect what it could do would it a pumpkin be. (221)

Antichrist

O Man, why do you gape? The Beast and Antichrist,[26]
Unless you are in God, are both in you confined. (225)

---

22. This elaborate image goes back to Bernard of Clairvaux's *De diligendo Dei* (On loving God), where it is developed in the concluding section.
23. Cf. RV. 17:2.
24. *Ebrietas spiritualis*, or spiritual intoxication, goes back to the biblical interpretation of the pentecostal miracle where the apostles were able "to speak in tongues" (Acts 2:13).
25. Cf. Mt 13:31f., 17:20.
26. Cf. 1 Jn 2:18–22.

BOOK ONE

Babel

Yourself you are a Babel;[27] if you don't venture out,
Eternally you stay in Satan's howling house. (226)

Anger

Anger hell's fire is; does it your heart inflame,
It surely will the Spirit's sweet resting-bed profane. (229)

Blessedness Is Easier To Achieve

I deem it easier to soar to Heaven high,
Than with the toil of sin in the abyss to pry. (230)

How the Soul Desires God

Lord, if you love my soul, then let her, pray, embrace you;
She surely never will for thousand gods forsake you. (234)

The Silent Prayer[28]

God far exceeds all words that we can here express
In silence He is heard, in silence worshiped best. (240)

God's Dwelling

My body, marvelous! God's dwelling has become;
So high in His esteem that equal it has none. (241)

---

27. Cf. Rv 17:3–5. Sandaeus's *Clavis* explains the concept under its own heading: "Babylonica captivitas. Mystice est servitus in mundo. Eadem soluta est liberatio a servitute mundi. S.Augustinus in tractatu in Psalmum CXLVIII" (The Babylonian captivity in the mystical sense is bondage in the world. It can be dissolved through liberation from this worldly bondage, as St. Augustine explains in commenting on Psalm 148). Probably the most famous modern use, and one Scheffler's contemporaries were surely reminded of, was Martin Luther's treatise of the same name; *De captivitate Babylonica* was one of the three fundamental treatises the reformer wrote in 1520, employing the image, polemically, of course, for the world and the institutional church.
28. Cf. Introduction, section 4.

God's Dwelling-Place

Christian, if you love Christ and have His gentleness,
Then God will find in you His dwelling and His rest. (243)

Love Is the Wise Man's Stone[29]

Love is the wise man's stone: It divides gold from mud,
It makes nothing of self and turns me into God. (244)

The Tincture

The Holy Spirit smelts, the Father does consume,
The Son the tincture[30] is, which gilds and does transmute. (246)

Goldness and Divinity

Goldness creates the gold, Divinity makes God.
Are you not one with it, you remain lead and mud. (249)

Infancy and Divinity

Since God revealed Himself to me as infancy,
I bow to infancy as to Divinity. (254)

How To Be Child and Father

I am God's child and son, and yet my child is He.
How can it ever happen that both these things should be? (256)

Nature Is Threefold

The Godhead is triune, as every plant reveals;
Sulphur, salt, mercury[31] are all in one concealed. (257)

---

29. The wise man's stone was indeed perceived by alchemists to enable the transmutation from nonprecious matters into gold.

30. The term *tincture* designates both the alchemistic process of mixing and the product. Cf. Introduction, section 4.

31. According to both Theophrastus Bombastus Paracelsus (1493–1541) and Jakob Böhme, these three elements were the three fundamental substances of all physical and cosmic matters. Cf. Introduction, section 4.

BOOK ONE

Divinity and Humanity

So much indebted is Divinity to man,
Without man It does lose heart, courage, and all sense. (259)

This Is the Day of Salvation

Arise, the bridegroom comes![32] And none shall he possess,
But the beloved bride who stands in readiness. (260)

The Wedding of the Lamb

The banquet is prepared,[33] the Lamb does show its wounds,
Woe to you have you not found God, Who is your groom. (261)

The Wedding Gown

The wedding gown is God,[34] His Holy Spirit love;
Wear it and you shall see recede your spirit's sloth. (262)

God Is Unfathomable

So rich the Godhead is in Its diversity
That It can never plumb Its own depth utterly. (263)

Creatures Are God's Echo[35]

Nothing is without voice: God everywhere can hear
Arising from creation His praise and echo clear. (264)

Unity in Multiplicity

Alas, that we do not, as the sweet forest birds,
Each utter our own note and lustily converge! (265)

---

32. Cf. Mt 25:6.
33. Cf. Mt 25:6 and 22:4.
34. Cf. Mt. 22:11.
35. The notion of every creature's being able to resound in God was very popular in sixteenth- and seventeenth-century poetry; in fact, a whole subgenre, "echo-poems," developed from it. Cf. Introduction, section 4.

The Mocker Counts for Nothing

The nightingale does punish not the cuckoo's tune,[36]
Whereas you show disdain, unless it sings like you. (266)

One Thing Alone Does Not Always Satisfy

My friend, if all together we utter but one tone,
What music would that be, all sung in monotone? (267)

Diversity Is Pleasing[37]

The more we let each voice sound forth with its own tone,
The more diverse will be the chant in unison. (268)

With God All Things Are One

The croaking of a frog to God appears as fair
As does the lark's sweet trill, which upward soars in air. (269)

The Voice of God

Creatures are but the voice of the Eternal Word:
It sings and sounds its self, in sweetness and in dread. (270)

Man Is God's Other Self

What God can ever desire in His eternity,
That He perceives in me as in His effigy. (272)

Man Restores Everything to God

Man, creatures love you so, it's you they are pressing toward;
Hastening to come to you, thus to attain their God. (275)

---

36. The nightingale, normally an image for the soul, is juxtaposed here with the cuckoo in reference to a fable where the ass had to judge on the competing birds and decided in favor of the cuckoo since he could not understand the nightingale's harmonies.
37. Cf. Introduction, section 2.

BOOK ONE

One Is the Beginning and End of the Other[38]

God is my final end: If I in Him begin,
He takes His being from me and I am lost in Him. (276)

The End of God

That God shall have no end, I never will admit,
Behold, He seeks my soul, that He may rest in it. (277)

God's Other Self

I am God's other Self, He can in me behold
What from eternity was cast in His own mould. (278)

His Precepts Are Not Hard

Man, if you live in God, and die to your own will,
How simple it will be His precepts to fulfill. (281)

In God Is the Best State

The morning stars praise God;[39] what does it profit me
Unless I too, O Lord, am lifted into thee? (282)

God Is above Holiness

Shout on, O Seraphim,[40] that which of you one reads;
I know that God, my God, much more than holy is. (283)

One Must Go beyond Thought[41]

What Cherubim may know will never bring me peace,
Outstrip I must all thought, the highest goal to reach. (284)

---

38. Cf. Introduction, section 2.
39. Cf. Ps 148:3.
40. Cf. Is 6:2–4. This phrase has a central place in the liturgy of the mass, introducing the "Sanctus," which precedes the transubstantiation.
41. Cf. Introduction, section 4.

The Knowing Must Become the Known[42]

In God is nothing known: He is undivided, One,
That which one knows in Him, one must oneself become. (285)

Without Why[43]

The rose does have no why; it blossoms without reason,
Forgetful of itself, oblivious to our vision. (289)

Leave It in God's Care

Who does adorn the lily? Who decks out the narcissus?
Why, Christian, are you then so overly solicitous? (290)

The Saints' Reward

What is the saints' reward? What ours after death?
It is the lily flower of purest godliness. (292)

It Must Be First in You

If you not Paradise first in yourself possess,
Believe me that you never will find to it access. (295)

The Closest Playmates

Not all is near to God; the Virgin and the Babe,
These two, and they alone, shall be God's playing-mates. (296)

The Children of God

Because God's children are to running so opposed,
They must be driven to it by God, the Holy Ghost.[44] (301)

To Halt Is To Walk Backward

In all matters divine, halt means calamity,
For backward you then walk into catastrophe. (302)

---

42. Cf. Introduction, section 2.
43. "Sonder waeromme," the Middle-High German version of "without why," was one of the basic formulae of medieval mysticism.
44. Cf. Rom 8:14.

Book Two

Love Is above Fear

The fear of God is good, better it is to love;
Still better in His love to be raised far above. (1)

Love Is a Magnet

Love like a magnet is, it draws me into God,
And what is greater still, it pulls God into death. (2)

The Light Is Not God Himself

Light the Lord's raiment is, but should you lose that light,
Know that you have not lost of God Himself the sight. (5)

Nothing Is the Best Comfort

Naught the best comfort is; without God's brilliancy,
Nothing can comfort lend in dark adversity. (6)

The Woman upon the Moon

Why are you lost in thought? The Woman in the Sun,
Who stands upon the Moon,[1] must first your soul become. (9)

The Bride Is the Most Cherished

Say what you will, the bride is the most cherished child,
Whom one finds in God's womb and in His arms enshrined. (10)

The Greatest Security

Slumber my soul and sleep,[2] in the wounds of your lover,
You will security and sweet repose discover. (11)

---

1. Cf. Rv. 12:1ff. The emblematic tradition depicting the moon as a reflection of the sun was quite prevalent at that time.
2. The notion of the "somnus/sopor mysticus" is traditional.

57

ANGELUS SILESIUS

God Withholds Nothing

Come drink and have your fill, all is for you and free;
Divinity itself shall then your banquet be. (17)

The Book of Life[3]

God is the Book of Life, inscribed therein I am
With the blood of His Lamb: Should He not love me then? (20)

The Center

If set straight in the center your dwelling-place shall be,
Then you see at a glance the whole periphery. (24)

You Are the Cause of Your Restlessness

No creature and no God can cause you such unrest;
Restlessness dwells alone, O Folly, in your breast. (25)

Freedom

How noble freedom is! Who has to it surrendered
Knows not of what a man who loves it is enamored. (26)

The Same

Who freedom loves, loves God; whose trust in God is placed,
Who rids himself of all, he with the gift is graced. (27)

Death and God

Death is the wage of sin,[4] God is true virtue's gain;
And if you win this not, the other you'll obtain. (29)

Essence and Accident

Eternal essence be! The world will fall away,
The accidental perish, essence alone will stay. (30)

---

3. Cf. Rv. 3:5 and *passim*.
4. Cf. Rom 6:23.

BOOK TWO

The Divine Savior

Who wants to savor God and will in Him inhere,
Should, like the morning star, to its own sun draw near. (31)

Proper Use Does Not Bring Loss

Man, if you say that things keep you from loving God,
Then you don't use the world in quite the way you ought. (34)

What Humanity Is

Would you like to inquire what is humanity?
It is (put in a word) superangelity. (44)

God Loves Himself Alone

Indeed it is quite true, God loves Himself alone
And whom His other Self can in His Son become. (45)

Who Is God Sees God

Because in its real nature, the true light I should see,
Itself I must become, or else this cannot be. (46)

Love Seeks No Profit

Man, if you love your God and profit thereby seek,[5]
You have not savored yet what love's true nature is. (47)

God Is Known by His Creatures

God is the hidden God, known to us by a sign,
As traced into His creatures who are but His design. (48)

God Loves Virginity

God drinks of Virgin's milk,[6] which does indeed prove clearly,
That true virginity is relished by Him dearly. (49)

---

5. 1 Cor 13:5.
6. Mary feeding the baby Jesus was a popular subject of religious paintings of that time ("Maria lactans").

ANGELUS SILESIUS

God Becomes a Little Child

Divine immensity is in a child confined.
Oh, how I wish to be a child within this child. (50)

The Inexpressible

You think that you may utter the name of God in time?
It is not even uttered throughout eternity. (51)

God Is, He Does Not Live

God is, essentially; He does not love and live,
As one of you and me, and other things, may speak. (55)

You Must Outgrow Yourself

If you outgrow yourself and leave behind all creatures,
Then you shall be imbued with the divinest nature. (57)

Of Loving

If naught you will and love, your will and love are good;
Who loves all that he wills, loves not that which he should. (60)

One Must Dwell in Both

My God, how cold I am! Help me to become warm
In your humanity's womb and in your Godhead's arms. (62)

Spiritual Voyage

The world my ocean is, the captain is God's Spirit,
My body is the ship, toward home the soul is steered. (69)

Purity

Most perfect purity is image-, form-, and love-less,[7]
Defies all attribute, as much as does God's essence. (70)

---

7. Another instance of apophatic mysticism (cf. note to 1:199). Sandaeus's *Clavis* poses
the question thus (290; Gies, 49): "DISQUISITIO: Quid sit nuditas mystica. RESPON-
DEO: Est omnium rerum externum, imo interiorum, formarum, ac imaginum absentia et
privatio" (Exploring Question: What might mystical nakedness be? I answer: It is the absence
and deprivation of all external things, and internal ones as well, of forms and images).

BOOK TWO

The Essential Man

A true, essential man is like eternity,
Which always stays untouched by externality. (71)

Who Sings with the Angels?

Who would with just one glance above himself aspire,
May join the Gloria of the Angelic Choir. (72)

God's Spiritual Temple

The portals of your city are wrought so pearl-fine,
A flash must be my spirit, your temple[8] and your shrine. (79)

Mount Olive

Should the Lord's agony redeem you of your sin,
Mount Olive you must scale and first become his kin. (81)

The Illumination

Soar up where lightning will encompass you with Christ,
And you dwell with the three, upon Mount Tabor's[9] heights. (84)

Surrender

The lightning of God's Son quickly transparent renders
The hearts which are to God entirely surrendered. (90)

---

8. 2 Cor 4:16.
9. Cf. Mt. 17:1–9. Mount Tabor, in connection with mystical illumination, occupies a central place in the pertinent imagery, as the entry in Sandaeus's *Clavis* shows (350/51; Gies, 48): "DISQUISITIO: Quid Mons Thabor in mystica disciplina denotat? RESPONDEO: Montem Thaborem habere mysticos, tanquam imaginem mentis altissimae . . . Thabor lucis accesionem quidam interpretantur. Si ergo . . . Petrus sumus et Jacobus . . . et Johannes, iam Christus ducit nos in montem nudae mentis nostrae. Ruusbroec . . . " (Exploring Question: What does Mount Tabor designate in mystical thinking? Answer: According to the Flemish mystic Ruusbroec mystics hold it to be the image of the highest disposition of mind . . . and they interpret it as the accession to the Light. As Christ led Peter, James, and John, so does he lead us onto the mountain of our spiritual nakedness).

Patience

Patience counts more than gold; it can conquer my God,
Take what He has and is, enclose it in my heart. (91)

The Most Secret Abandon

Abandon pleases God; but to leave God Himself
Is an abandonment which few can comprehend. (92)

One Is the Comfort of the Other

God is the light of lights, the Savior is the sun,
The Virgin is the moon, myself their joy I am. (94)

Safe Is Best

Flee, my dove, oh, flee; rest in the soul of Christ;
Where else can you so safely be hidden and disguised?[10] (98)

Externals Do Not Bring Comfort

What does it profit me if Gabriel hails the Virgin,[11]
Unless he brings to me the very selfsame tidings? (102)

You Must Expanded Be

Come and expand your heart, so God can enter in:
You shall His Kingdom be and He shall reign therein. (106)

The World Does Not Pass Away

The world is vanishing! It does not pass away,
It's just obscurity which God does there erase. (109)

Creatures Are Good

You do lament that creatures cause nothing but torment;
Not so; they do for me a path to God present. (114)

---

10. Cf. Sg 2: 12 and 14.
11. Cf. Lk 1:29.

BOOK TWO

The Best Society

Society I shun, unless, of course, the Child,
The Virgin, Lamb, and Dove are all together joined. (116)

One Drinks and Eats God

If you are divinized, you drink and eat your God;
This is forever true, with every piece of bread. (120)

The Spiritual Vine[12]

A vine I'm in the sun, the Father plants and feeds it,
The fruit that springs from me is God's eternal Spirit. (122)

Grace Becomes Nature

Why should a Christian be devout and just and free?
You ask wherefore a lamb cannot a tiger be.[13] (126)

They Must Be Gilded

O Christian, let your deeds be deep in gold immersed,
Or God will not esteem you or your works on earth. (130)

Abandonment

Go out and God comes in; die, and you live in God;
Be not, it will be He; be still, God's plan is wrought. (136)

Self-Naughting

Nothing raises you up as does annihilation;
The more brought low you are, the more divinization. (140)

Eternity

What is eternity? It is not This nor That,
Not Now, no Thing, no Naught; it is I know not what. (153)

---

12. Cf. Jn 15:1ff.
13. Classical topos for peace in paradise.

ANGELUS SILESIUS

A Star Precedes the Sun

I do not ask too much if thousand suns there are;
If only I can be in Jesus' eyes a star. (154)

It Is up to You

O Man, don't miss your chance, it is for you to see:
Leap up, through God you can mightiest in Heaven be. (155)

One Perceives God in Oneself

What my God's form may be, yourself you should perceive,
Who views himself in God gazes at God indeed. (157)

Spirit Is alike To Essence

My spirit is like being, it knows essentially
From where it has emerged and came initially. (159)

Spirit Can Never Die

Spirit lives by itself, even if it lacks light,
(As happens with the damned) it still can't lose its life. (160)

One Lives Best Interiorly

What is my spirit's spirit, and my essence's essence,
That is what I have chosen for myself as dwelling. (161)

The Weak Must Wait

My poor, sweet little bird, can you yourself not fly,
Then patiently sit still, until you can arise. (173)

All Do Not Have To Face Judgment

The men who here below are one with Christ in God,
Conquered death and judgment, in bliss, as these were naught. (177)

BOOK TWO

Everything Rests on You and Me

There are but you and I; and when we two are not,
The heavens will collapse, God will no more be God. (178)

Man Is Nothing, God Everything

I am not I nor you: yet you are I in me,
And so my God I pay all homage sole to thee. (180)

To God Everything Is Present[14]

No future and no past! What is about to be
Forever was in God perceived essentially. (182)

The Cherubim Looks Only At God

Who puts his gaze down here only on God alone,
Will be as Cherubim near the divinest throne. (184)

The Son and Throne by Grace

Out with the shadow throne: The sole, incarnate Son
Is now in me that Self, my conciliation throne. (185)

One Should Not Tempt God

Be modest, chaste, and still; who walks without concern,
The Majesty Divine will hurl down and burn. (186)

One Must Avoid the Forbidden

Who never eats the fruit the Father has forbidden
Will not a foot be banished from the Garden of Eden.[15] (191)

Light Will Reveal It

Go, call the morning star: for when the day breaks forth,
It truly will reveal what fair is and what coarse. (194)

---

14. Cf. Introduction, section 2.
15. Cf. Gn 3:3.

ANGELUS SILESIUS

Man the Other God

Tell between me and God the only difference?
It is (put in one word) nothing but otherness. (201)

Pure Emptiness of Spirit

Pure emptiness of spirit is like a noble vase,
Which in it nectar[16] has: and having, knows not what. (209)

Divine Holiness

Man, if you are in earnest, then without falsity
You may holy and just like your Creator be. (210)

What Is Sanctity?

True sanctity of spirit is like a glass of gold
Wholly polished and pure; observe what you behold. (211)

From and Toward

Two words I like to hear, and they are from and toward:
From Babel[17] and myself, toward Jesus and toward God. (213)

All Works Are of Equal Value

There is no difference: Should they the dung be raking,
Angels like it no less than rest and music-making. (214)

One Must Orient Oneself

Who turns his glance toward East[18] and there awaits his God,
In him will soon arise the gracious morning's dawn. (215)

---

16. In Greek mythology the drink of the gods, making them immortal.
17. City on the river Euphrates; seen as the epitome of perversion. Cf. Rv 14:8.
18. The East has a broad spectrum of religious significance in Christianity; e.g., churches were usually erected in this direction.

BOOK TWO

Usury Is Necessary

Enrich yourself, O Serf: for when the Lord arrives,
The usurer alone will in His realm survive.[19] (222)

How God Loves Chastity

Chastity holds with God as much esteem and power,
As thousand lilies[20] are above a tulip flower. (223)

Derision Brings Joy

Derided and forsaken, enduring pain and toil,
Denuded, not possessing, my life is filled with joy. (244)

Silence Resembles the Eternal Naught

Nothing resembles naught than to be silent, still:
For silence nothing seeks but what He wills, my will. (248)

The Devil Sees Not through Light

Man, wrap yourself in God, abscond into His Light:
I swear that you will thus escape the devil's sight. (249)

It Must Flow from God

Should first my lamp spread light and purest rays bestow
The oil must then from you, my dearest Jesus, flow.[21] (251)

The Seraphic Life

With love to walk and stand, love breathe and speak and sing
That is to spend your life as do the Seraphim. (254)

---

19. Cf. the simile in Mt 25:14ff.
20. The lily as the emblem of triumphant virtue, in particular of chastity, has a long literary tradition.
21. The spiritual interpretation is based on the parable of the five foolish and the five wise virgins (Mt 25:1ff.).

ANGELUS SILESIUS

The Five Spheres in God

Five spheres there are in God: serf, friend, son, bride, and spouse.
Who goes beyond becomes oblivious of those. (255)

Only the Pure Shall See God

O Man, be newly born! So fair you must become
Before God's countenance, to equal Christ, His Son. (256)

Book Three

For the Crib of Jesus

This wood more precious is than throne of Solomon.[1]
For there enfolded lay God's true Eternal Son. (1)

On the Stable

O pilgrim, enter here; the stall of Bethlehem
Exceeds by far the town, the fort Jerusalem.
You gain good shelter here, for the eternal Babe
Is found here with His bride, His mother and His maid. (2)

To the Virgin Mary

O noble Lady, speak, was it humility
That chose you to conceive God, Who's infinity?
Or was it something else? For I would like to know
How to be maiden, bride, God's mother here below. (3)

A Sigh

One placed God upon straw when He a man became;
If only I had been that very straw and hay. (4)

The Simplicity that Honors God Most

How simple we must grow, how simple they who came!
The shepherds looked at God before all other men.
He sees God nevermore, not there, not here on earth
Who does not long within to be a shepherd first. (6)

The Blessed Silence of the Night

Note, in the silent night, God as a man is born
To compensate thereby for what Adam had done.[2]

---

1. Cf. 1 Kgs 10:18–20. In alchemy, the throne of Solomon stood for the highest level of perfection.
2. Cf. 1 Cor 15:45ff. Scheffler also knew about the theosophic speculation about the first ("Protoplast") and the second ("Kadmon") Adam.

71

If your soul can be still as night to the created,
God becomes man in you, retrieves what's violated. (8)

To the Shepherds

Answer, my dear people, what was it that you sang
When you entered the stable and with a trembling tongue
Adored your God, a child? I'd also like to sing
A pastoral of praise to Jesus sweet, my King. (9)

God Immersed in Man

God drinks humanity's milk, leaves His divinity's wine.[3]
How could He then not be immersed in His mankind? (11)

It Carries and Is Carried

The Word who carried all,[4] the very God, the Old,
Must here a little girl with tiny arms enfold. (12)

I Am the Cause

Tell me, my dearest child, is it for me you cry?
Ah yes, you glance at me, it surely must be I. (13)

The Best Hymn of Praise

Chant, all you angels, chant! With hundred thousand tongues
To this most blessed Child is scarcely homage done.
Oh! If I only were without a voice and tongue
I know that I could sing straightway the sweetest song. (15)

He in Me, I in Him

Know, God becomes a child, lies in the Virgin's womb,
That I would grow like Him, His Godhead may assume. (16)

---

3. Cf. Sg 5:1.
4. Cf. Jn 1:1ff.

72

BOOK THREE

God-Man

Reflect! God becomes me, entering earth's misery,
That I enter His realm and may become as He. (20)

The Circle within the Point[5]

When God lay hidden in the womb of a young virgin,
It happened that the point fully contained the circle. (28)

For the Crib of Jesus

Here lies the precious Babe: first fruit of Virgin's womb,
Angels' delight and joy, men's richest price and boon.
Should he your Savior be and lift you into God,
Then, man, stay near the crib and make it your abode. (30)

Heaven Becomes Earth

Heaven humbles itself, toward earth makes its descent;
When will the earth arise and become heaven-bent? (32)

The Sweetest

Sweet is the honeydew, and sweet is the new wine,
Sweet is the heavenly bread, manna of Israelites.[6]
Sweet is what Seraphim from the beginning chant,
Yet sweeter still, dear Lord, your five wounds sweetness are. (35)

God in Love

God's love means me alone, it is for me He burns,
He dies of sheer dismay if I for Him not yearn. (37)

The Best Station Is under the Cross

The blood that from the Lord's beloved wounds does flow
Is the most precious dew He will on us bestow.

---

5. Cf. note to 3:48.
6. Cf. Ex 16:14ff. The food given by Jahweh to the Jews crossing the desert from Egypt.

73

If you would sprinkled be and bloom unfadingly,
Then you must never think His holy Cross to flee. (39)

To Those Who Flee the Cross

Does it astonish you that you can never rest,
Not steadily repose upon our dear Lord's breast?
Those most beloved are, who throughout grief and pain
In torment, anguish, death, closest to Him remain. (41)

To the Sinner

Awake, dead Christian, see how our Pelican[7]
Besprinkles you with blood and water of His heart. (42)

Inscription on the Tombstone of St. Mechtild[8]

Here lies the maiden of God, the flowering Mechtild,
With whom He has His heart so often calmed and stilled. (45)

The Same

Here lies God's bride, Mechtild, a child so very fair
That Father, Son, and Spirit have fallen in love with her. (46)

On the Tombstone of St. Francis[9]

Here lies a Seraphim; I wonder how the stone,
With such a fiery blaze, could still remain a whole. (47)

---

7. Already in ancient liturgy this bird was thought to be the perfect symbol of piety (and Christ) because it was alleged to feed its young with blood plucked from its own breast.

8. Probably Mechtild of Hackeborn (1242–1299). Scheffler had in his library a copy of the *Liber specialis gratiae*, a devotional text containing revelations of this saint and of her sister, Gertrud the Great. Scheffler's handwritten glosses in this copy indicate a particular liking for these saints.

9. The "seraphic" saint (1182–1226) received the stigmata in 1224. Cf. Chapter 13 of the *Life of St. Francis* by Bonaventura in the Classics of Western Spirituality series (trans. and ed. Ewert Cousins, 1978).

The Great within the Small

My God, how can this be? My spirit, nothingness,
Longs to devour you, vast everlastingness. (50)

St. Lawrence[10]

Oh, do not wonder why amidst the fiery blaze
St. Lawrence's mouth stayed open, showing no dismay.
The flame that had, within, his very heart enflamed
Caused him to outwardly not feel the coal's hot flame. (62)

St. Augustine[11]

Because your heart's on fire with God, O Augustine,
More fitting it would be to name you Seraphim. (64)

Of Mary Magdalene

The tears which you observe often at the Lord's feet
Are those the Magdalene does there profusely weep;
They are her melted heart. She does so deeply mourn
That she can body and soul not into tears transform. (65)

Of the Blessed Virgin

That body virginal, it never could be dead
Nine months within itself, enclosed our heavenly bread.[12]
No cedar tree decays; nor were it fitting, sure
That God His ark should leave outside the temple door. (66)

---

10. St. Lawrence (+ 258) was tortured to death in Rome by being roasted on a grill. In supreme irony he is reported to have admonished the executioners to have him turned so that the other side could be properly treated, too! His courage must have been outstanding since his martyrdom induced many high-ranking Roman nobles to convert to Christianity.
11. Aurelius Augustinus (354–430), influential church father, whose emblem is a flaming heart pierced by two arrows.
12. Reference to the "shewbread" of the jews (Ex 25:30) and the Eucharist. The images following in the text refer to attributes ("the cedar of Lebanon" and the "arca foederis") of Mary named in the *Lauretanian Litany*.

75

Beatitude

What is beatitude? A flood of joy exalted,
A gazing upon God, a love that never falters,
The sweetest Jesus Kiss, the longed-for life immortal,
Not for an instant be from the Beloved parted. (68)

The Spiritual Sulamite

God is my Solomon, I am His sulamite;[13]
When I adhere to Him, He will in me delight. (78)

To Everyone His Own

Sailors speak of the sea, the hunters of their hounds,
The miser speaks of gold, the soldier of his wounds.
Me, since I am in love, nothing so much befits
As having God and love forever on my lips. (82)

Roses

Roses I like to see, for they are white and red,[14]
Covered with thorns they are, like my blood-bridegroom, God. (84)

You Should Be White and Red

I wish from my soul's depth a heart, my Lord and God,
White in its innocence, and from Your blood red-robed. (85)

Unfolding like a Rose

Your heart receiveth God with all His Kingdom holds,
When you but turn toward Him and like a rose unfold. (87)

You Must Blossom Now

Awake, O wintry Christian![15] May greens before your gate.
If now you grow not verdant, death surely be your fate. (90)

---

13. The name of the beloved of King Solomon praised in the love poems attributed to him in the Song of Solomon or Song of Songs (cf. 6:13).
14. Cf. the description of the beloved in Canticle 5:10.
15. In tone and imagery in the tradition of a popular Easter hymn.

BOOK THREE

The Secret Rose

The rose is like my soul, the thorn is carnal lust,
The spring is like God's grace, His wrath is cold and frost,
The blossoms are good works, the thorns contempt of flesh,
With virtue it is adorned, in heaven it seeks rest.
In the fullness of time, when spring it has become,
God's rose it will then be, the only chosen one. (91)

Without Dissimulation, No Sin

What is it, not to sin? Don't on the question dwell,
Listen to what the flowers in silence have to tell. (98)

A Pure Heart Gazes at God

The eagle fearlessly turns to the sun its gaze[16]
As you do at God's flash if your heart is unstained. (99)

The Way to the Creator

Alas, O mortal Man, do not set such vast worth
On baser appetites and colors of this earth.
The beauty of the creature is nothing but a bridge,
Which leads to the Creator, Who Himself Beauty is. (102)

Justice Makes Blessed

To attain blessedness, wear silk as white as snow,
As lustrous as you can, body and soul to clothe. (103)

The Human Heart

God, devil, and the world all wish to enter me;
Of what great lineage my noble heart must be. (111)

---

16. In the emblematic tradition, the eagle is the only bird who can face the sunlight directly and, by doing so, in fact increases his vision instead of going blind.

The Temple of God

I am the temple of God and of my heart the shrine;
The Sacred Mystery, if pure and undefiled. (113)

Metamorphosis

The Beast becomes a man, man will an angel be,
The angel God, once we recover totally. (114)

The Cornerstone Is Best

We seek the stone of gold and leave the cornerstone,[17]
Through which we could have rich, healthy, and wise become.
(117)

God Lacks Something

One says God needs no gifts, for He is lacking naught.
Why then should it be true that He needs my poor heart? (123)

The Secret Kingdom

I am a mighty realm, my heart is the high throne,
The soul reigns as its Queen, the King is God's own Son. (131)

A Heart Can Enclose God

Quite without measure is the Highest, as we know,
And yet a human heart can wholly Him enclose. (135)

Love Is Dead

Alas, oh, love is dead! How could it perish thus?
No one has cared for it: It simply died of frost. (138)

---

17. A prominent biblical image, e.g., Ps 118:22 ff., Mt 21:42.

BOOK THREE

God Dwells in Calm

O Man, becalm your heart; God is not in great sound,
In tremblings of the earth,[18] or conflagrations found. (142)

The Power of the Soul

So great is the soul's might, God must to it assent
That He may never leave without its own consent. (146)

God Wishes To Be Alone

Lock God into your heart, let nothing enter in;
He then must dwell with you and be enjailed therein. (147)

God Is My Point and My Circle[19]

God is my center, if I do encompass Him,
My circle He becomes, I am enclosed in Him. (148)

What God's Lover Desires

Three things that I would be: radiant as Cherubim
As tranquil as are Thrones, on fire as Seraphim. (165)

The Godhead

The Godhead is a source from which all things do rush
And then return to it. An ocean It is thus. (168)

God Is the Only Why

Not you, nor friend or foe, solely God's honor alone
Shall now your single why and final cause become. (174)

---

18. Allusion to 1 Kgs 19:11f.
19. Sandaeus's *Clavis* (243; Gies, 101) places this traditional image in the following context: "DISQUISITIO: Quid connotatum denotet immergo mysticum? RESPONDEO: Mysticus . . . considerat se, tum ut centrum, Deum ut spheram cuius medium in ipso aspiciente est. Circumferentiae autem terminus nullus est" (Exploring question: What mystical connotation does immersion denote? I answer: The mystic literally sees himself as the center of the divine ball whose circumference has neither beginning nor end).

God's Eternal Work

What did God before time, on His eternal throne?
In love with His own Self, beget His only Son. (175)

The Long Torment

The martyrs have obtained, ah, in a glorious way,
After a brief death to see God's everlasting day.
We suffer agonies throughout our whole life's length.
And what torments us so? It is concupiscence. (177)

About Love

If all our earthly loves always in sadness end,
Should then our hearts not be on Divine Beauty bent? (179)

God Knows Not of His Beginning

So you would like to see God's life in length revealed?
Silence! It is so long, from Him it is concealed. (180)

About God

God never was before, and never again will be;
Hereafter He's alone, as He before has been. (181)

Constancy Is Required[20]

The highest good required to gain felicity,
If we stand in good grace, is loving constancy. (183)

You Must Have Patience

Have patience, my dear soul! Robes of magnificence
Cannot be worn by you, while in this wilderness. (184)

---

20. Constancy as unperturbed uprightness was the primary virtue of humanists of a stoic persuasion.

BOOK THREE

Man Is Great before God

How boldly we are viewed! The highest Seraphim
Are covered before God; nude we may come to Him. (203)

The Saints Measure God

Who plumbs the depth of God? Who knows how high He flames?
Who measures length and breadth?[21] The company of saints. (214)

Evil Knows No Rest

Oh, wonder! All aspires to obtain its rest;
And yet an evil man can find therein but dread. (221)

The Virgin Must Also Be Mother

Virginity is noble, yet mother you must be,
Or else you are a field robbed of fecundity. (224)

Christ's Threefold Future

The future of the Lord was, is, and too shall be
In flesh, in spirit, and when we His glory see. (227)

The Precious Pearl

The Lord compares His realm to a single pearl fine,
That it be highly valued and preciously enshrined.[22] (231)

Never Come to a Halt

If you wish to arrive, never stop on the way,
One must from light to light forever forward strain. (232)

---

21. Cf. Eph 3:17–19.
22. An allusion to the simile of Mt 13:45–46.

ANGELUS SILESIUS

The Threefold Kiss in God[23]

Three ranks are kissing God: The maids fall to His feet,
Virgins draw near to Him, His gentle hand to kiss;
The bride so wholly is wounded by His great love
She lies upon His breast, kissing His honeyed mouth. (235)

The Distinguishing Mark

The devils revile God, the beasts pay Him no heed,
Men do proclaim their love, the angels gaze on Him
Ever unwaveringly. Hence one can clearly tell
Whom one may give the name: Angel, man, beast, or devil. (236)

Thrice Wise[24]

Three Wise Men offer God three precious gifts in me:
The soul, the gold of love; the body, myrrh of pain,
The spirit, frankincense of devotion, as its fee.
Oh, that I ever could thus three times wise remain. (240)

The Wondrous Birth

The Virgin is a crystal, her Son celestial light;
Wholly she is pierced by Him and yet stays unimpaired. (242)

The Miraculous Exchange

Oh, marvel! God's own Son grows young in midst of joy
And must in sheerest fright pass again from this world.
We are born in midst of tears, and then we take our leave
With laughter, if we wholly within His spirit live. (243)

---

23. Scheffler follows the famous threefold division of kisses put forward by St. Bernard in his sermons on the Song of Songs: the kiss of the foot of spiritual neophytes ("incipientes in via purgativa"), the kiss of the hand of the illuminated ("proficientes in via illuminativa"), and the kiss of the mouth of the united ones ("perfecti viae unitivae"). Cf. particularly sermons 6–8 in *Works II*, *Song of Songs I*, trans. Kilian Walsh OSCO (Kalamazoo: Cistercian Publications, 1980).
24. The magi of Mt 2:1–12.

BOOK THREE

Be on Your Guard

Virgin, be on your guard; once you become a mother,
The adversary seeks straightway your child to smother. (244)

The Ineffable Reversal

All things are now reversed: The castle is the cave,
The crib becomes the throne, the night brings forth the day,
The Virgin bears a Child; Reflect, O Man, and say
That heart and mind must be reversed in every way. (245)

On the Crib

The crib I now consider my precious jewel-shrine,
For Jesus lives in it, who is my ruby[25] fine. (246)

The Birth of the Pearl[26]

The pearl is from dew, within the shell's own depth
Generated and born, by which is clearly told
What you fail to believe: The dew's the Holy Ghost,
The pearl Jesus Christ, and my soul is the shell. (248)

---

25. The emblematic connotation was either that of "burning love" or of the healing properties of blood.

26. The explanation of the pearl's origin dates back to antiquity. It was often allegorically related to Jesus' birth from Mary. For the extensive tradition in literature, and in arts and crafts, cf. Sigrid Barten, ed. *Die Muschel in der Kunst. Von der Renaissance bis zur Gegenwart* (Zürich: Museum Bellerive, 1985), pp. 10ff.

Book Four

God Becomes What He Never Has Been

God not made manifest, comes into time to be
What never He has been through all eternity. (1)

The Secret Nazareth and the Spiritual Annunciation

Mary and Nazareth, Gabriel, who tidings brought,
They are my soul and heart, a light renewed by God.
My heart, when it becomes a richly flowering border,
The soul, when it belongs to the chaste Virgin's order,
Do in this garden dwell; the light of grace rekindled
Is God's eternal Word, uttered within my spirit. (4)

The Child Jesus at His Mother's Breast

How shabbily God's Son is welcomed on the hay,
Surrounded as He is by sheerest poverty.
He barely notices as long as He may rest
Upon His sweetest mother, quite close upon her breast. (5)

Eve's Fall Is the Cause of the Incarnation[1]

God's own eternal Son enters this wilderness
And nourishes Himself now from a Virgin's breast.
Who caused Him this great woe, how did that come to be?
A woman who had fallen, the root of it was she. (7)

The Name of Jesus

The name of Jesus is an oil poured out and spilt,[2]
It nourishes and shines, the soul's own woe it stills. (8)

Felicity

No man has ever known perfect felicity
Until his otherness is drowned in unity. (10)

---

1. Theologically, this concept of the "felix culpa" (the blessed sin of Adam and Eve, which made redemption and salvation through Christ possible) features extensively in the Easter liturgy.
2. Cf. Sg 1:3.

87

ANGELUS SILESIUS

God Sends the Great within the Small

In waste God hides the gold, accept what He may send,
The great within the small, though we don't comprehend. (14)

To the Lord Jesus

I draw to you, O Lord, you are my sunlight's splendor,
Which all illuminates, gives warmth, and life does render.
If you draw near to me, as to your earth, and come,
Then will my heart quite soon a verdant spring become. (17)

God Is the Goal of Every Virtue

God is each virtue's goal, its impulse and its crown,
He is its only why, reward and sole renown. (18)

Worldly Pleasures

The pleasures of this world, which end in agony,
How is it you surrender to them so totally? (20)

The Unknowable God[3]

One knows not what God is. Not spirit and not light,
Not one, truth, unity, not what we call divine.
Not reason and not wisdom, not goodness, love, or will,
No thing, no no-thing either, not being or concern.
He is what I or you, or any other creature
Has never come to know before we were created. (21)

Love

Love is alike to death, annihilates the senses,
My heart it breaks as well, the spirit's drawn from hence. (29)

God Is above All Gifts

I pray, it's true, O Lord, quite often for your gifts,
But know that I would have yourself much more than this.

---

3. Cf. Introduction, section 4.

BOOK FOUR

Give me eternal life, or grant me what you want,
If you don't give yourself, then you have given naught. (30)

The Blessed Leisure

Mary is at His feet, St. John leans on His breast,[4]
They both do nothing else, but savor God at rest.
How blessed is their state! Could I in such peace dwell
I surely would not stir if all the heavens fell. (31)

The Depth, Breadth, Height, and Length of God[5]

In wisdom God is deep, in mercy He is wide,
High in omnipotence, long in eternal life. (35)

The God-Abandoned Are Already Blessed

A man who is abandoned to God in all his ways
He may already now to blessedness be raised. (39)

Maria[6]

These are the Virgin's names: a throne, God's canopy,
Ark, fortress, tower, house, tree, garden, mirror, fount,
The sea, a star, the moon, the rosy dawn, a mount:
She is another world, thus she can all these be. (42)

On the Wounds of Christ

I look upon Christ's wounds as wide celestial gates
And know that I can enter through the five safest places.
How may I come straightway to stand close to my God?
I shall through feet and hands enter the heart of love. (46)

---

4. Two well-known scenes (Lk 10:39 and Jn 13:23).

5. A free interpretation of Eph 3:17–19. The traditional interpretation, according to Sandaeus's *Clavis* (169; Gies, 113) goes as follows: "Quid est Deus? Longitudo, latitudo, sublimitas et profunditas. Longitudo: aeternitas; latitudo: caritas; sublimitas: potentia; profunditas: sapientia" (What is God? Longitude, latitude, sublimity, and profundity. Longitude stands for eternity, latitude for charity, sublimity for power, and profundity for wisdom.)

6. Most of these shortened images (throne = sedes sapientiae/throne of wisdom, etc.) are taken from the *Lauretanian Litany* (= the litany devoted to Mary).

ANGELUS SILESIUS

The Cross

The Cross I chose to be my treasure of high value,
My body's plow it is and also my soul's anchor. (48)

Christ's Glory in This World

The scepter is the reed, the thornbush is the crown,
The nails are the crown jewels, a deadly cross the throne.
His blood a gown of purple; murderers, the men at arms,
The court made up of rabble, knaves and rogues vassals are,
The goblet bitter gall, music contempt and scorn:
This is the royal glory which here on earth has God. (49)

The Place of Skulls[7]

Is this the Place of Skulls? How can it happen then
That rose and lily here in fadeless beauty stand?
And there, the Tree of Life, the fount of the four rivers?
Yes, it is Paradise; Whatever be its name,
Skull place or Paradise: I value them the same. (50)

Love Has Invented It

That God is crucified and can be wounded, hit,
That He the shame endures He is afflicted by,
That He such anguish bears and He can come to die,
Do not astonished be: Love has invented it. (52)

The World Is Made in Spring

In spring the world was won, renewed, regenerated,
Thus rightly you can say, in spring it was created. (54)

The Secret Ascension

If upward you can soar and let God have His way,
Then this has in your spirit become Ascension Day. (56)

---

7. The literal translation for the Hebrew "Golgotha." In the German text, a note by Scheffler designates the rose and the lily as "Mary and John."

BOOK FOUR

Spiritual Inebriation[8]

The Spirit's like new wine, see the disciples all,
Like men inebriate, swept away and enthralled
By both its heat and strength; thus it remains true still
That the disciples had of sweetest wine their fill. (57)

The Lost Sheep[9]

I am the sheep that's lost and sadly went astray
And now can by itself not find the rightful way.
Who will show me the path, so that I won't succumb?
If Jesus only came to carry me straight home. (59)

The Prodigal Son[10]

Return, O prodigal Son, to God, Who is your Father,
Or you will come to grief by hunger (His disfavor).
Had you a thousand times inflicted on Him shame,
If only you returned, His embrace would be the same. (60)

Of Mary Magdalene[11]

What does the Magdalene think, confessing openly
At the feet of the Lord her guilt so publicly?
Oh, do not wonder why, behold her radiant gaze
And how consumed she is by her love's fiery blaze. (66)

Sin

Sinning is nothing but turning from God one's face
And having turned it thus, turning it toward death. (69)

The Word of Highest Solace

The very highest solace that I in Jesus find
Will be when He shall say: Come forth, my blessed child.[12] (75)

---

8. Cf. note to 1:210.
9. Cf. Mt 18:12–24.
10. Cf. Lk 15:11–32.
11. Traditionally the name of the sinful woman of Lk 7:37ff.
12. Mt. 25:34.

ANGELUS SILESIUS

My Best Friend and Foe

My closest friend, my body, is also my worst foe;
However well it means, it does delay me so.
I hate and love it both, and when the end appears,
From it I tear myself with equal joy and tears. (79)

Trumpets[13]

Trumpets I like to hear; my body to their noise,
From earth shall rise again and be to me rejoined. (83)

The Song of Songs

The king does lead his bride for wine into the cellar,[14]
That she may choose the one that most delights her palate.
If you would be God's bride, He will deal with you thus;
Nothing He has Himself, He not to you entrusts. (88)

Virtue

Virtue, the wise man says, is its own best reward.
If he means here and now, I am not in accord. (90)

The Figure of This World

The figure of this world is transitoriness;
Why do you put such worth in its magnificence? (96)

Both Are Good

Heaven is my desire, the earth is also dear;
For while I am still upon it I may to God draw near. (97)

Of Lilies

Whenever I see lilies, I always suffer pain
And yet I also feel abundant joy again.

13. Cf. 1 Cor. 35ff., particularly verse 52.
14. Cf. Sg 2:4.

The pain is caused by me, for the jewel I mourn,
Mine from the beginning, in Paradise my due.
The joy derives from this, that Jesus has been born,
Who has invested me with all this joy anew. (98)

Man Is Thrice Angelic

The Throne Prince rests in God, on Whom the Cherubim gaze,
For Whom the Seraphim melt in sheer love away.
I recognize all three in one soul singly dwelling
And thus a holy man must three times be angelic. (108)

Remorse Arrives Too Late

While God walked on this earth, He barely knew esteem;
Now that He dwells above, it is to be bewailed
That higher honor has not to Him here been paid.
So foolish is the world, nothing has it foreseen. (115)

The Cask Must Be Clean

Clear out your heart's cask well; if sediments appear
Then God will not pour in His wine precious and clear. (119)

Beholding Heaven

To him who beholds Heaven, all creatures are as naught.
But why? He lives alone in his Creator, God. (120)

Animals Partake of Heaven

One says no animals can enter in God's realm.
Whoever are the four, who near His Throne do dwell?[15] (121)

God Does Not See above Himself

God cannot see above, hence nothing do presume,
Or you might run the risk to vanish from His view. (122)

---

15. The four evangelists' emblems, often pictorially grouped around God's throne, are: a man with wings (Matthew), the lion (Mark), the ox (Luke), and the eagle (John).

ANGELUS SILESIUS

The Inscrutable Cause

God is all to Himself, His Heaven and His bliss.
Why are we then created? We cannot answer this. (126)

To Those Who Love the World

The soul, since it is formed for all eternity,
Will tire of finite joys and ever restless be.
Thus I am quite amazed that you should set such worth
On all that fleeting is and passing on this earth. (128)

No One Speaks Less than God

No one speaks less than God outside of time and place;
He makes eternally a single utterance. (129)

About Justice

Justice has disappeared! Where has it gone? To Heaven.
But why? It was too frightened by this earthly Babel.
What could have happened though? Down it would have been cut.
The world would long ago have weakened it and struck! (131)

Loss and Gain

Death is but gain to me, a long life merely loss,[16]
And yet I thank my God, Who on me it bestows.
I grow increasingly, as long as on this plane:
Therefore my life to me is verily a gain. (132)

The Power of Return

If you, my soul, return to what has been your source,
You'll be what you have been, that which you honor and love. (134)

The Brook Becomes the Sea

Here I still flow in God, as does a brook in Time,
There, I shall be the sea of beatitude divine. (135)

---

16. Cf. Phil 1:21.

BOOK FOUR

The Spark in the Fire

Who is it who can tell the spark within the fire?[17]
And who, once within God, can perceive what I am? (137)

The Blessed Submergence

If you know how to launch your ship onto God's sea,
Oh, what a blessed fate, submerged in it to be. (139)

The Noblest Prayer

The noblest prayer will a man so much transform
That he becomes himself that which he does adore. (140)

The Sweetest Tone

There is no sweeter tone heard in eternity
Than when my heart with God resounds in harmony. (143)

The New Birth

Quietude of spirit makes you into a Throne,
Love into a Seraph and peace into God's Son. (144)

I Am More Noble than Seraphim

I, man, am far more noble than all the Seraphim,
I can be what they are; they never what I am. (145)

Man's Vastness Cannot Be Measured

Who is it that can say that he can measure me,[18]
If God in me does walk, who is infinity? (147)

---

17. The favorite image of Meister Eckhart expressing divinization. The *locus classicus* for this image is to be found in his (German) *The Book of "Benedictus": The Book of Divine Consolation* (cf. the edition in the Classics of Western Spirituality series, trans. and ed. Edmund Colledge and Bernard McGinn, 1981, p. 221): "And so I say that likeness, born of the One, draws the soul into God, as he is one in his hidden union, for that is what 'One' signifies. Of this we have a plain example: When material fire kindles wood, a spark receives the nature of fire, and it becomes like pure fire." Cf. also Introduction, section 4.

18. Cf. 2 Cor 6:11–13.

ANGELUS SILESIUS

The Soul Dilated

What causes heart and soul to be so much dilated?
It is the love of God which so has them created. (148)

The Highest Divine Service

To be like unto God is highest divine service,
To have the form of Christ in love, in life, in bearing. (150)

True Wisdom

The truest wisdom, that to which we can aspire,
Is to be joined with God, to be with love on fire. (151)

God Is Everywhere Undiminished

O Being without match! God is outside my sphere,
And yet contained in me, quite there and also here. (154)

How God Dwells in Man

Closer than soul to body and reason to the mind
God's essence is to you, wholly your domicile. (155)

The Same

God far more dwells in me than if the entire sea
Would in a tiny sponge wholly contained be. (156)

God Is within and around Me

I am the vase of God, He fills me to the brim,
He is the ocean deep, contained I am in Him. (157)

The Great Is Hidden in the Small

Circumference is in a point, the fruit rests in the seed,
God in the world does dwell, wise who will there Him seek. (158)

All in All

How saw Saint Benedict all in a (sun-)ray revealed?[19]
See, all is hidden in all, and is therein concealed. (159)

God's Splendor Is Everywhere

No speck so tiny is, no spark can be so dim,
The wise man does not see God's splendor deep within. (160)

The Hidden Source

Who would have thought of this! The darkness brings forth light,
The something comes from naught, death does engender life. (163)

God's Portraiture

I know God's Portraiture; he left it in disguise
In all His creatures fair, for you to recognize. (164)

God Still Creates the World

God still creates the world: Does reason this defy?
Know that with Him, before and after don't apply. (165)

God's Action and Repose

God never was at work nor in repose; (observe!)
His work is His repose and His repose His work. (166)

The Highest Peace

The peace most highly prized, which keeps the soul delighted,
Is knowing itself to be close with God's will united. (173)

Abundance of the Blessed

God fills the cup of Saints so overflowingly
That they more in the wine than it in them will be. (174)

---

19. St. Benedict (480–547) once had a vision of the whole world under one sunbeam.

ANGELUS SILESIUS

The Wondrous Match

Oh, what a wondrous match! The God of majesty
Has wed a beggarmaid, the soul, His Queen to be. (175)

Astonishment at Familiarity with God

It is astonishing that I—dust, ash, and mud—[20]
May on familiar terms be with the highest God. (177)

Dawn and Day of the Soul

While we still move in time, God does as dawn appear;
But in beatitude, He shall be noonday clear. (180)

About the Blessed[21]

The soul beatified knows naught of otherness,
With God she is a light, an utter gloriousness. (181)

One Should Choose the Giver

O Man, leave all God's gifts and always rush toward Him,
If you cling close to gifts, you find no rest therein.[22] (187)

After This There Will Be No Works

O Man, act while you can, to earn eternal bliss;
No works can you perform, after this time has ceased. (208)

---

20. The series of images is clustered as it is in the liturgy of Ash Wednesday.

21. Scheffler's handwritten entry in Sandaeus's *Clavis* under the headings "Transformatio/Deificatio" (354; Gies, 92) reads: "(Spiritus cum Deo) unum efficitur, unus Spiritus, una anima, unum esse, una felicitas; alteritatem namque non recipit, Dionys. Carth. de vita solit. 1.2.cap. 10" (To be unified in Spirit with God effects one Spirit, one soul, one whole, and one blessedness, for no otherness can be conceived, according to Dionysos the Carthusian's [d. 1471] *On solitary life*).

22. This is an almost literal translation of a passage of one of the main sources for Sandaeus (247; Gies 34): Blosius, *paradisam animae fidelis*, cap. 10, "ubi agit de indifferentia in adversis . . . Neque enim in donis Dei, sed in ipso Deo quiescere debemus" (According to Blosius's *Paradise of the faithful soul*, chapter 10, whose subject is indifference in adverse circumstances . . . We have to find rest not in God's gifts, but in God Himself).

BOOK FOUR

The Conceiving Soul

The soul that's virginal and naught but God conceives,
Can pregnant be with God as often as it pleases. (216)

The Sign of God's Bride

The bride does fall in love with no one but her spouse;
If you love aught but God, how can you be espoused? (218)

God's Wandering Canopy

The soul in which God dwells is (Oh, wondrous delight!)
A wandering canopy of the eternal light. (219)

God Should Be Known by the Soul

As a master knows his house, a prince his tenancy,
The soul should know her God, Who is her legacy. (223)

How One Achieves Unity

When man starts to withdraw from multiplicity
And turns his face toward God, he enters unity. (224)

The Majesty of Man

I am (Oh, honor high!) son of eternity,
Myself by nature King, a throne of majesty. (226)

Book Five

As All Numbers Derive from One, Creatures Come from God[1]

Just as all numbers have their only source in one,
Creatures originate from God Who is the One. (2)

God Is in Everything as Unity Is in Numbers

Just as does unity in every number dwell,
So God, Who is the One,[2] in all things lives as well. (3)

The Naught Counts Nothing if Placed in Front

The creature that is naught, if before God it's stated,
Counts naught; place it behind and it is highly rated. (5)

In the One All Is One

All is one in the One; when two returns to One,
It has essentially a single one become. (6)

The Mystical Number

Ten is the royal number,[3] made up of one and naught.
When God and creature meet, then does it come about. (8)

God's Palace

God is His own high throne, the heavens are His hall,
The forecourt paradise, the universe his stall. (10)

Damnation Is Grounded in Essence

Could one who had been damned the highest heaven attain,
He still would feel forever hell's agony and pain. (15)

---

1. Scheffler's knowledge of cabbalistic speculation of numbers derived from a series of publications from the library of his friend Abraham v. Franckenberg. The main source was Robert Fludd's *Philosophia Mosayca*, 1638, I, 2 dealing with the ideal existence of God.
2. Cf. Mk 12:29.
3. The German "Kronzahl" has a number of meanings; here it refers to the importance of a "perfect" number as known from the commandments, etc.

Chastity Is a Womb

Chastity is a womb, which no one can pry open,
To know what is its core, may no stranger hope for. (22)

Time Is Not Fast

You say that time moves fast, but who has seen it fly?
Contained and fixed it rests, in God's Eternal mind. (23)

One Does Not See God with One's Eyes

Our gazing upon God is not by sense perceived,
The vision is within, not outwardly received. (24)

God Becomes Alike to Us

God gives you what you take, yourself you pour the draught;
It will be what you wish as wine flows from the cask. (26)

The Crossroads to Eternity

The crossroads are down here: which way to pull the rein?
The left brings you but loss, the right nothing but gain. (27)

What God Does All Day

At daybreak God goes out, at noon He is asleep,
At night He is awake, evenings He walks at ease. (28)

One Must Contemplate the Depth from the Heights

Indeed God is abyss, yet whom He shows His face,
He must ascend the peak of the eternal range. (29)

When God Likes to Dwell with Us

God, whose sweet bliss it is to dwell within our breast,
Comes then most readily when we our house have left. (33)

BOOK FIVE

God Can Do More, Not Less

There's nothing God can't do; stop laughing and don't mock,
Though He cannot make God, He can indeed make gods. (35)

Many Gods yet One

God one, yet manifold, how can they coexist?
Clearly because they all in one as One subsist. (36)

God Looks at the Root

God values not your deeds, but how they are performed;
He does not view the fruit, only the root and core. (37)

God Gathers Figs from Thistles

God gathers figs from thistles, from thorns He gleans the wine,[4]
When He your sinful heart to penance does incline. (38)

The Saints Are Never Sated[5]

That they are never sated makes all the saints rejoice;
Oh, what a happy hunger, Oh, what a blessed thirst! (39)

Christ Is like a Rock[6]

Who stumbles upon Christ (who is a granite stone)
Lies shattered; grasp Him and be led securely home. (40)

The More You Know of God, the Less You Can Comprehend Him

The more you know of God, the more you will confess
That what He is Himself, you can name less and less. (41)

---

4. This is an ironical inversion of Lk 6:44: "For of thorns men gather no figs."
5. Cf. Jn 7:37.
6. Cf. Mt 21:42–44.

ANGELUS SILESIUS

God's Justice

Behold how just God is; could there a greater be,
He'd pay him honor first and bend to him His knee. (43)

You Are the First Sinner

Silence, O Sinner, stop! Accuse not Eve and Adam,
Without that incident, it's you who would have done it. (46)

One Cannot Accomplish It without the Other

Two must accomplish it; I cannot without God,
God cannot, without me, make me escape my death. (48)

The Fairest Wisdom

O Man, leave your conceit, seek not too high to rise:
The fairest wisdom is not to be overly wise. (49)

God Is Not Virtuous

God is not virtuous; from Him virtue emerges,
As rays do from the sun, water from ocean surges. (50)

Everything Is Modeled after God

God is from origin of all things the Creator
And is their model too, hence nothing is inferior. (51)

You Must Yourself Be Heaven

To Heaven you can't go, stop all the agitation,
Unless you are, before, yourself a living heaven. (52)

The Nature of Vice and Virtue

Virtue rests in repose, vice rears right up in strife:
Conflict vice has within, virtue a joyous life. (54)

God Does Not Punish Sinners

God does not punish sinners; sin sounds its own discord,
Is fear, toil, torture, death, as virtue is reward. (55)

There Is Perfection in Everything

Nothing imperfect is; the ruby's like a pebble,
The frog[7] is just as fair as Seraphim, the angel. (61)

With God There Are No Years

For God a thousand years are but a day that's passed.[8]
Hence there's no year with Him. How hard is this to grasp. (63)

The Distance to Heaven

Christian, do not believe that Heaven is so distant;
The path that leads to it takes nothing but an instant. (67)

The Difference between Evil and Good

A will o' the wisp is evil, a good man is a star;
The first burns on itself, the star is flash from God. (69)

Not Much Is Needful

Christian, you want not much for eternal blessedness,
You need a single plant, it is abandonment. (70)

God is Equally Close to Everything

God is to Beelzebub[9] near as to Seraphim,
Only that Beelzebub does turn his back on Him. (72)

---

7. The frog has a long literary tradition as an (Easter) symbol of the resurrection, which, in the sixteenth and seventeenth centuries, was reflected in emblems.
8. Cf. Ps 90:4.
9. German name for the biblical reference to the highest of demons (cf. Mt 12:24).

God Cannot Remove Himself

God never does withdraw; His works come to no halt;
If you don't feel His force, yourself must be at fault. (73)

In Hell There Is No Eternity[10]

Reflect on this with care: God is eternity;
With the devil in hell, eternal time will be. (74)

Nothing Lasts without Joy

Nothing lasts without joy. God in Himself has joy,
Or else His essence would like grass be scorched, destroyed. (75)

The Cross Is Safest

One lies most blissfully on suffering, pain, distress;
But who will gladly choose on such a bed to rest? (79)

The Cross Is Love's Most Cherished Place

Tell me where love is found in her most cherished place?
Where to the Cross she's bound, for her Beloved's sake. (82)

The Creator within the Creature

Creation is a book,[11] and who knows how to read
Shall find his sovereign Lord clearly in it revealed. (86)

---

10. Cf. Introduction, section 4.
11. An old metaphor, which in Sandaeus's *Clavis* (263; Gies, 118) is described as follows: "Liber Dei. Ita mundum indigitant mystici . . . Blosius, *Paradiso animae fidelis*, cap. 28, universus iste mundus velut quam liber est, Dei digito scriptus, in quo singulae creaturae, tanquam singulae litterarum figurae sunt! Docet deinde in eo legere quidem . . . spiritualem ac mysticum legere ac intelligere gloriam Conditoris . . . " (The Book of God. Mystics address the world according to Blosius's *Paradise of the faithful soul*, chapter 28, thus: This world is a universe and a book, written by the hand of God, in which there are creatures and letters. You have to read in it . . . read what is spiritual and mystical, and comprehend the glory of God).

BOOK FIVE

The Best Book

Too many books cause stress; who reads one thoroughly
(I mean the book of Christ) gets well eternally. (87)

One Must Gain It Here

Down here it must be gained. I surely cannot see
How he who wins no realm could there a sovereign be. (89)

There Is No Temporality in God

An instant is so short, yet I would like to say
That God had not been long before night was and day. (90)

When God Made the World

When God had made the world, what year did we write then?
No other than the first of His own origin. (91)

God Does Not See Before

God sees nothing before, thus you are lacking sense
If with your simple mind you measure Providence. (92)

What God Is to the Blessed and to the Damned

God to the blessed is an ever-joyful guest
And to the damned He is a burden in excess. (95)

God Cannot Steer the Will

Nothing stronger than God! And yet He can't prevent
That I should wish and want to what I don't consent. (98)

God Died More than Once on the Cross[12]

It is not the first time, God to the Cross was nailed,
It was already Abel in whom He had been slayed. (103)

---

12. A traditional prefiguration, based on Gn 4:3ff.

ANGELUS SILESIUS

One May Steal Heaven

Who does good works in silence, stores wealth in secrecy;
No doubt he has God's Kingdom stolen quite skillfully. (105)

Faith Alone Is an Empty Cask

Faith without love alone[13] (if I remember right)
Is like an empty cask; it sounds, has naught inside. (108)

All Creatures Follow the Creator

If you possess your God, all else will follow suit,
Man, angel, sun and moon, air, fire, earth, and brook. (110)

Not All Goodness Is Good

Not all goodness is good; always keep this in sight,
What burns not in love's oil is a deceiving light. (112)

Nothing Has More Splendor than the Soul

My soul is filled with splendor, nothing can equal it.
Why? Jehovah Himself changed Himself into it. (121)

About God, There Are More Lies than Truths[14]

What you affirm of God is much less truth than lie,
For what you state of Him, to creatures does apply. (124)

The Soul Is above Time

The soul, eternal spirit, is itself above time:
It lives already here an everlasting life. (127)

The Inward Life Does Not Need the Outward One

Who has recalled his senses to the interior life
Hears what one cannot say, sees in the darkest night. (129)

---

13. Cf. 1 Cor 13:12.
14. Cf. Rom 1:18–20.

BOOK FIVE

Man Is Great

Man must be great indeed! God does his nature take,
Which He would never do for all the angels' sake. (131)

The Wise Are Not Grieved

The wise do never grieve in sorrow, woe and pain;
They do not even pray to be released again. (133)

The Wise Are Always Content

All things the wise men please; to be tranquil and still,
If it is not their own, it surely is God's will. (136)

God Also Listens to the Mute

O Man, if you to God with words for grace can't pray,
Then mutely Him approach, and He will not delay. (137)

The Wise Man Never Misses His Goal

The wise man never misses, he always hits the goal;
His aim is very sure and called the will of God. (140)

The Worldly Goings-On Are a Tragedy

Do not begrudge the world its false felicity,
All its performances are but a tragedy. (141)

In Heaven One May Do as One Pleases

Man, tame a little bit, while still on earth, your will:
In Heaven you may surely its every wish fulfill. (142)

Christ Causes Strife and Enmity

You think that Christ will bring but love and unity?
No, truly, where He is are strife and enmity.[15] (145)

---

15. Cf. Mt 10:34.

In God All Shall Be One

In God all shall be one. The humblest of His Kingdom
Will be to Christ Our Lord and to His Mother equal. (147)

In Eternity Everything Happens at the Same Time

There in eternal life reigns simultaneity,
No after, no before, no temporality. (148)

All Men Must Become as One

Multiplicity God shuns; therefore He draws us in,
That all He has created in Christ be one to Him. (149)

Each Rejoices in the Other's Beatitude

In Mary's beatitude and that of her sweet Son,
I shall rejoice as fully, as had I they become. (151)

In Heaven Each Rejoices in the Other

The greatest saint will be in such a state of bliss
Because of me as truly as I rejoice in his. (153)

Who Seeks Peace Must Overlook a Lot

Man, if with what you own you are so much concerned,
You never will acquire a lasting peace on earth. (154)

Christ Is the First and the Last Man

The first and also last is solely Christ Himself:
From Him all comes to be, in Him all comes to rest. (155)

The Passion of Our Lord Did Not End on the Cross

The Passion of Our Lord did not end on the Cross:
By night and also day He suffers still for us. (159)

BOOK FIVE

Man Must Fulfill Christ's Passion

Man, you must be Saint Paul[16] and in yourself fulfill
What Christ has not yet done, the wrath divine to still. (160)

The Sinner's Praise

The praise that God the Lord from unjust ones receives
Is much less loved by Him than a dog's barking is. (162)

God Receives Only the Lambs[17]

God wills that all should come to His divinest Son,
And yet He will receive none other than the Lamb. (164)

Sin Brings about Some Good

Sin brings some good: It does with the devout conspire,
That they may before God to nobler heights aspire. (167)

How To Appear at Court

Who wishes to approach Majesty without fear,
He first of all must clean and deeply bowed appear. (169)

The Virtues Are Entwined

The virtues are together so closely intertwined
That he who one possesses may all the others find. (171)

What the Saint Does, God Does in Him

Himself God acts in saints, performs their actions here:
He walks, stands, lies, sleeps, wakes, eats, drinks, is of good cheer.
(174)

God Creates Nothing New

God nothing new creates, though it may to us seem;
Past is eternally what we by future mean. (179)

---

16. Cf. Col 1:24.
17. Cf. Mt 25:33 and Rv 14.

God Enters Only Chaste Hearts

The bridegroom of your soul desires to come to you:
Green forth! He will not come until the lilies bloom. (180)

The Nature of a Christian

Evil repay with good, if wronged do no one slight,
Thank for ingratitude, that is the Christian life. (183)

One Saint Sees Himself in the Other

Reflect that every Saint himself in all will see;
If all were not as one, how could this ever be? (184)

Selfishness Is the Cause of All Evil

Pour out and you find rest; merely in selfishness
Originates all woe, war, persecution, stress. (186)

The Highest Bliss Save God

The highest bliss in Heaven (save God) shall surely be
Hearts opened to each other in pure transparency. (187)

Many Kinds of Blessedness

Many mansions[18] there are, manifold blessedness;
Oh, if you only were for one in readiness! (188)

Eternally God Is in Love with His Beauty

God's beauty is so radiant, unutterably bright,
That He eternally feels rapture at its sight. (189)

Blessedness in Time

The Saint is never needy; in time he does possess,
From pleasing God so well, eternal blessedness. (190)

---

18. Jn 14:2.

BOOK FIVE

One Discovers God in Leisure

God comes more readily if He finds you in leisure
Than if you spend yourself in strenuous endeavor. (195)

God Has All Names and None

Indeed one can name God by all His highest names
And then again one can each one withdraw again. (196)

Love's Subject

The true subject of love is but the supreme good;
If one loves aught besides, one is a thorough fool. (199)

God Lacks Nothing

God works continually, a thousand joys He would
Pour into you at once, if suffer it you could. (205)

The New Creature

Man, you shall only be the newly fashioned creature
Once Christ's own piety becomes your spirit's nature. (208)

New and Old Love

Our love, when it is new, sparkles as does young wine;
The mellower it grows, the clearer it will shine. (210)

Seraphic Love

The love we are accustomed seraphic here to call,
One barely can, it is so still, perceive at all. (211)

God's Throne Rests in Peace

In whom the Majesty should rest as on a throne,
Must in Jerusalem dwell, high up on Mount Sion. (213)

God Is All to All

God's everything to all; he loves in Seraphim,
He reigneth in the Thrones, gazes in Cherubim. (215)

God Is like to a Fountain

God is like to a fountain. He flows so tenderly
Into His creation and yet remains within. (216)

In God Everything Is Beheld Simultaneously

Friend, when you behold God, at one glance you shall see
What without God you can't see in eternity. (217)

God Cannot Will Evil

God never wills what's evil; willed He adversity
Or wished the sinner's death, God He would cease to be. (218)

Do Not Remain a Mere Man

O Man, be more than man, attain the highest peak:
In the Kingdom of God, but gods shall be received. (219)

One Must Suffer before One May Rejoice

If you hope to enjoy God through infinity,
You must first in this world His death's own consort be. (222)

Equanimity[19]

The Saint deems it the same: If God lets him lie ill,
He thanks Him just as much as he were sound and well. (227)

---

19. A central concept of Ignatian spirituality well known to Scheffler. Sandaeus's *Clavis* quotes in direct reference to the Ignatian Exercises (246): "Debemus absque differentia nos habere circa res creatas omnes, prout libertati arbitrii nostri permissum est: ita (quod in nobis est) ut non quaeramus sanitatem magis, quam aegritudinem . . . " (We must have a discerning attitude in relation to all things created as much as they are dependent on our free judgment: thus it is in our power that we do not desire health more than sickness . . .).

The Evil Is Yours

The good derives from God, hence it is His alone;
The evil comes from you, that you may claim your own. (230)

The Most Beautiful Thing

Nothing in either world as fair as I can be,
For God, Beauty Itself, has fallen in love with me. (232)

When Man Becomes God

Before I ever was, I have been God in God;
I shall be that again, if to myself I'm lost. (233)

Everything Returns to Its Origin

The body out of earth, again to earth must come.
The soul, derived from God, will it not God become? (234)

Eternity Is Innate to Us

Eternity is to us so native and profound
We must eternal be, whether we will or not. (235)

Mine and Yours Are Damned

Nothing casts you as deeply into hell's very jaws
As two detested words, and they are mine and yours. (238)

God Has No Other Model but Himself

Why God created us the image of His own?
I say because He has simply no other one. (239)

When Man Is Wholly Restored

Tell me when man will be to God wholly restored?
When he the model is from which God had him formed. (240)

117

ANGELUS SILESIUS

To Love, All Is Submissive

Love reigns as Sovereign; even the Trinity
To love submissive is throughout eternity. (241)

God's Nature

Love is God's very nature, He can't act otherwise;
Hence if you would be God, love also without why. (243)

God Has No Name but Love

There is no name that would do justice to our God;
One therefore calls Him Love,[20] which is with treasures fraught.
(245)

God Cannot Hate

Man, comprehend this well: God cannot hate His creatures;
He cannot even hate the very devil's features. (247)

Three Kinds of Sleep

Three kinds of sleep there are: The sinners sleep in death,
The feeble ones in nature, and those enamored in God. (248)

Three Kinds of Birth[21]

The Virgin bears the Son of God externally,
I inwardly in spirit, the Father eternally. (249)

God's Birth Persists Forever

God does beget His Son: He does this timelessly,
And hence this birth persists throughout eternity. (251)

---

20. Cf. Jn 4:8.
21. In epigrammatic form, this is the theme of the most famous sermon of John Tauler on the meaning of Christmas as a threefold birth (cf. Sermon 1 in the *Johannes Tauler: Sermons* volume Classics of Western Spirituality series, trans. Maria Shrady, intro. Josef Schmidt, 1985).

BOOK FIVE

Each Belongs to Its Origin

The water in the well, the rose upon its stalk,
The flame amidst the fire, the soul is best in God. (253)

The Soul without God

A sheep without a shepherd, a body that is dead,
A fountain without spring my soul is without God. (254)

Pain Is Followed by Joy

War does resolve in peace, joy follows after strife,
Condemning your own self brings you a blissful life. (255)

To Look Backward Is To Be Lost Again

When you from Sodom[22] flee, the Judgment to escape,
Salvation will depend on never looking back. (256)

God Becomes Me, Because I Was He Before

What I am, God becomes, takes my humanity;
Why has He acted thus? Because I once was He. (259)

God Is in All Things Undefiled

Nothing shares in God's nature that is inferior here,
And yet, God's nature must in demons too appear. (261)

The Depth of Humility

Humility can plunge much deeper than a well,
It values itself less than all the foes in hell. (262)

One Must Taste Hell

Christian, you must be once in hell's abysmal fire,
Endure it while on earth, not after you expire. (263)

---

22. Cf. Gn 19:26. Because Lot's wife, against the express order of God, looked back, and she became a pillar of salt.

ANGELUS SILESIUS

Who Goes Past God, Sees God

O Bride, if you should seek the bridegroom's face to view,
Go past God and all things, He'll be revealed to you. (269)

All Salvation Is from God

I become God through grace; through love He becomes me,
And thus my eternal good solely derives from Him. (270)

If You Cease Being Man

If you cease being man and empty have become,
Then God Himself is man and will your burdens don. (271)

God's Countenance Bestows Bliss

The countenance of God draws like a magnet stone:
To catch one glimpse of it, eternal bliss bestows. (272)

Suffering Is More Useful than Pleasure

Man, if you only knew the worth of suffering,
You would have chosen it ahead of anything. (275)

The Saint Does Not Act because of the Law

The Saint performs his works not to obey the law.
He acts from purity and sheerest love of God. (276)

The Just Have No Law

The law is for the wicked; if laws were never wrought,
The just would always love their neighbor and their God. (277)

What Was in the World's Place before It Came To Be?

What was then in this place before God made the world?
He was that place Himself, with His Eternal Word. (279)

BOOK FIVE

God Cannot Measure Himself

God is so high and vast, had He Himself to fathom,
He would, though God, forget the number of His measure. (280)

What Is Most Marvelous, Good, and Beautiful in God

Most marvelous in God is His high Providence,
The best long-suffering, most beautiful His justness. (281)

Why God Has Joy and Rest

Because God is triune, He does have joy and rest:
Rest comes from unity, joy from the threefoldness. (283)

Simplicity Must Possess Wit

Simplicity I praise, which God endowed with wit;
If it should lack wit though, the name would it forfeit. (286)

The Nature of Simplicity

Simplicity means this: to know nothing of guile
And on good works alone to humbly set one's eye. (287)

Virtue without Love Lacks Value

Virtue naked and bare can't endure before God,
With love it must be decked, that fair it may be thought. (289)

Beauty Derives from Love

Beauty derives from love; even God's countenance
From it originates, or it would radiance lack. (292)

The Greater the Love, the Greater the Blessedness

The measure of all bliss one does by love assess;
The more one has of love, the more one will possess. (295)

ANGELUS SILESIUS

One Cannot Love God without God

O Man, if God did not His own Self love in you,
You never could in love give Him His proper due. (297)

Love Knows No Fear

Love never knows of fear and can't extinguished be;
God first would have to die to His Divinity. (298)

Love Is Closer to God than Reason

Love rushes unannounced before God's Majesty,
Reason and sophistry must in his forecourt be. (307)

Accessibility

How accessible God is! The peasant maid He taught
As much as He did you the art of kissing God. (308)

What Delights the Soul Most

The most delightful news that my soul can receive:
To be eternally bride at the wedding feast. (309)

God's Kiss

The divine Bridegroom's kiss is sensitivity
To His sweet countenance and His benignity. (310)

The Soul Is Powerless without God

As lovely as the lute[23] does vibrate by itself,
As lovely sounds the soul which God does not impel. (311)

Charity Opens the Gates of Heaven

Be on familiar terms with tender charity,
The gatekeeper she is to high felicity. (314)

---

23. As an emblem, the lute stood for a balanced character.

BOOK FIVE

The Evangelical Shepherd[24]

The Shepherd is God's Son, the Godhead desert is,
Myself I am the sheep, whom He first sought and kissed. (316)

How One Peers into Heaven

One needs no second sight to peer straight into Heaven;
Turn from the world your face and see, it will then happen. (318)

The Highest Beatitude

The highest beatitude to which I can aspire
Will be the taste of God,[25] how sweet He is to savor. (319)

Tranquility of Soul

Tranquility of soul consists in this alone,
To be united whole to God, a oned one. (321)

Blessedness Is the Highest Good

The highest good alone does offer blessedness.
Why is it then forsaken for what is clearly less? (322)

The Crowning Virtue

The virtue that does crown lasting felicity
Is (Oh, hold fast to it!) unswerving constancy. (324)

Differentness of Soul

The sinner's soul lies down, the penitent's is raised,
And the soul of the just stands ready for the race. (326)

---

24. Cf. Jn 10:11–18, and Mt 18:12–14.
25. According to Sandaeus's *Clavis* (224/4; Gies, 57), "Gustus mysticus est Divinae dulcedinis interna perceptio" (Mystical taste is the inner foretaste of divine sweetness). The "odor of sanctity" played a great role in distinguishing the corpse of, and in the devotional practice of venerating, the saints.

ANGELUS SILESIUS

God Is Not Grieved by Sin

Indeed God's grieved by sin in you as His own son,
In His Divinity, He feels nothing therefrom. (328)

The Whole Trinity Assists

Omnipotence attracts, wisdom renders advice,
Goodness comes to my aid to win eternal life. (329)

How God's Voice Is Heard

The voice of God is heard: Listen within and seek;
Were you but always silent, he'd never cease to speak. (330)

What Is Not Done in God Does Not Please Him

God must beginning be, the middle and the end,
If you would please Him well by works of your own hand. (331)

Where Man Arrives when Annihilated in God

In God annihilated, I shall arrive again,
Where from eternity I have forever been. (332)

The Longer Eternity, the More Impenetrable

Eternity's vast sea, the more it's navigated,
The vaster it becomes, the less it's penetrated. (338)

The Godhead Is Unfathomable

How deep the Godhead is, no one may ever fathom;
Even the soul of Christ in its abyss must vanish. (339)

God Himself Must Earn Merit

That I the highest God have taken for my groom,
He has deserved since He humanity assumed. (340)

BOOK FIVE

Where Time Is Longest

The farther away from God, the deeper steeped in time;
Therefore a day in hell continues for all times. (341)

How One Acquires Divine Courtliness

If at God's highest court you wish to be received,
Then you must go to school first with the Paraclete.[26] (342)

The Spiritual Organ[27]

God is the organist, we are His instrument,
His Spirit sounds each pipe and gives the tone its strength. (343)

How To Measure God

One cannot measure God; yet one can measure Him
By measuring my heart; He is possessed therein. (348)

You Must Arouse Yourself

Christian! You must awake, through God, from your deep sleep;
If you don't rouse yourself, you'll stay fixed in your dream. (350)

Interiorly, All Senses Are as One

The senses dwell in spirit as one sense and one use;
Who sees God savors Him, feels, smells, and hears Him too. (351)

God's Sight Inebriates

God's countenance makes sated. If you could see His light,
You would be drunken-reeling, so dazzling is that sight. (353)

---

26. The Greek word (= advocate) is one of the titles of the Holy Spirit (e.g., Jn 14:16).
27. This allegory is, according to Sandaeus's *Clavis* (317; Gies, 33), taken from a (non-authentic) text by John Tauler (Inst., cap. 11): . . . "quae sit resignatio sonora? . . . In hac autem dulcissima diversarum vocum melodia Spiritus Sanctus Organiste gerit officium, et animae vires . . . sunt fistulae: angeli vero sancto huius organi folles calcant" (What is the resounding indifference? . . . In this sweetest of melodies of different voices, the Holy Spirit holds the office of the organist, the powers of the soul are the pipes, and the angels the organ-blowers).

ANGELUS SILESIUS

Why the Saints Are Not Equal

God does His works through nature, which always is diverse;
Thus one Saint will be grieved, the other will rejoice. (355)

The Holy Trinity Compared to the Sun

The body is God-Father, and God the Son the light,
The rays the Holy Spirit, from both He does derive. (359)

God Is Everything

All that your soul desires, from God it will receive;
If it seeks all outside, it comes to mortal grief. (370)

For Whom God Cannot Obtain Release

If you die without God, nobody can prevent,
Not even God Himself, to hell your being sent. (371)

The Bride Should Be the Groom's Equal

I need be wounded. Why? Because with painful wounds
The Savior has been found, Who's my eternal groom.
What use is this to you? Not fitting is it to see
That bride and groom should not each other's equal be. (372)

The Heart Most Blessed

A pure heart beholds God, a holy one savors Him,
One that is deep in love, He wishes to abide in.
How blessed is the man who is bent on things above,
So that his heart will be pure, holy, and in love. (373)

Book Six

How God Dwells in the Holy Soul[1]

If you should ask how God the Word in you does dwell,
Know that it is like suns flooding the world with light
And like a bridegroom coming in the night
And like a king enthroned in his realm,
A father with his son, a master in his school,
And like a treasure hidden from our sight
And like an honored guest in robes of white
And like a jewel in a crown of gold,
A lily in a flowery field,
And like sweet music at an evening meal.
And like the oil of cinammon ignited
And like a host in a pure shrine,
A fountain in a garden of cool wine:
Tell me, where else clad in such beauty he is sighted? (1)

The Secret Hart and Its Source[2]

The hart runs off to seek a cooling hidden spring,
So that it then may be refreshed and calmed therein.
The soul, in love with God, is rushing toward the source,
From which the purest stream of life comes flowing forth.
The source is Jesus Christ, Who with His bracing draught
Imbues us with true faith, restores us from sin's wrath.
If you drink freely from this Fount and are revived,
Then, holy soul, you have at blessedness arrived. (12)

The Holy Soul

A new Jerusalem, a castle all completed,
A realm no enemy will ever have defeated,
A maiden who was raised as high as any goddess
This, Virgin, is your soul when she is God's beloved. (14)

---

1. A series of popular biblical similes (line 3 = Mt 25:6; line 6 = Mt 13:44; line 9 = Sg 2:1 and 6:2).
2. Cf. Ps 42.

ANGELUS SILESIUS

The Son Carries His Father's Name

Tell me, what name was chosen finally by God
For those He had adopted in His Son as sons?
You ask and call Him God, therefore you must confess
That He must name us gods,[3] and surely nothing less. (15)

The Wise Man Seeks No Worldly Honors

The wise man does not seek through honors elevation;
Honor enough it is to be God's close relation. (25)

The Sinner Becomes Mud

The holy man ascends becoming God in God,
The sinner plunges down, becoming dung and mud. (29)

Man Must Do His Part

Stand upright, be erect! How can God raise you up,
If you with all your might choose to the earth be stuck? (31)

A Worm Puts Us to Shame

A silkworm[4] labors hard that it may learn to fly,
Whereas you choose instead upon the ground to lie. (32)

The Open Eye Can See

An open eye can see, if you shut yours, my child;
Then you shall not see God, and shall become mole-blind. (36)

Nothing Shines without The Sun

Without the light of sun, the moon is roughly shaped,
Rough, too, without the sun, becomes your own soul's face. (37)

---

3. Cf. Ps 82:6; Jn 10:34.
4. A popular emblem denoting a selfless person.

BOOK SIX

Who Remains Askance Is Not Part of the Whole

The sun gives life to all, and makes the planets dance,
How can you play your part if you remain askance? (42)

Who Disappears, Is No More

The sinner is no more. Why? I can see him clear!
If you had the true light, you'd see him disappear. (43)

What Decays Comes to Nothing

What steadily decays cannot stand still or stop,
Rushes toward the abyss and disappears in naught. (44)

Stubbornness Tears Itself Away from God

What's torn off from the body is not kissed by the head;
Remember, stubborn sinner, to Christ you won't be wed. (45)

What Is Separate Has No Share in the Whole

A leaf that has been shed, a sour drop of wine,
Tell me what share it has in either tree or vine? (46)

The Despicable Fall

Hold out world, devil, flesh; a Knight you are, O Christian;
A wretched thing it is to fall before a villain. (52)

Victory Follows the Battle

Christian, no one has triumphed and with it comfort won
Who not before in battle the foe has overcome. (54)

The Greatest Fool

Christian, where you can see a man who's bent on hell,
Then, without any doubt, a fool you name him well. (64)

131

ANGELUS SILESIUS

What It Is To Be Lost

What is it to be lost? Ask the sheep which was lost,
And then ask the lost bride of the eternal Spouse.[5] (78)

Eternal Perdition

That lamb is wholly lost that never is reclaimed;
The soul not found by God can never be regained. (79)

God Does Not Seek What Is Eternally Lost

God finds not what He seeks? He seeks eternally—
Not what has torn away in temporality. (80)

The Will Causes Loss

The will does make you lost, the will does make you found,
The will does make you free, fettered, and also bound. (82)

Eye and Heart Do Not Suffer Anything

The heart is like the eye: a tiny little grain,
When it is in your heart, already causes pain. (102)

Burdened One Cannot Advance

The sailor in a storm throws ballast overboard;
Burdened with gold you hope to enter Heaven's court? (103)

All for All

Beatitude is all. Who wants to touch the all
Will have to, here and now, dispense with all for all. (105)

Negligence Does Not Attain God

You say that you will see God and His light some day;
O Fool! You never shall, you must see Him today. (115)

---

5. A combination of two biblical images (Mt 18:12–14; Sg 3:2f.).

BOOK SIX

Who Does Not Desire Will Not Receive

Who longs not mightily to see God's face revealed,
Throughout eternity it stays from him concealed. (116)

Without Lovesickness There Is No Love

Delay does always grieve. If God does cause no pain,
Then I shall not believe your heart to be aflame. (117)

The Foolish Nonsaint

A Saint you will not be and yet wish Heaven to gain!
O Fool, only the Saints shall enter Heaven's gates. (137)

Spiritual Uncouthness

You put on finery to go to the King's Court,
Yet unadorned you dare to stand before your God? (138)

To the Insolent

You call yourself so humbly a worm before God's Son.
You, worm, wish to assume by insolence His throne? (143)

Sadness Is Followed by Glory

Who eats his bread with sorrow during the early morning
Shall have an evening feast, God's everlasting glory. (147)

Who Is Sated Here, Cannot Eat There

Why doesn't gluttony at the divine feast appear?
It can't, because it has gorged itself too much here. (148)

God Is a Merchant

God sells His merchandise when He His Heaven offers;
What does He sell it for? The arrow of a lover.[6] (151)

---

6. The secular image of Amor's arrow is given a spiritual meaning.

ANGELUS SILESIUS

The Closer to the Goal, the Surer the Win

The closer to the goal, the surer is the win;
If you aim for God's heart, you must draw close to Him. (155)

What You Intend Is Intended for Yourself

What you wish for your neighbor, that you ask for yourself.
If you don't wish his good, you ask for your own death. (164)

Give What You Desire

Man, you demand of God the whole of His vast realm;
If you are asked for bread, you tremble and turn pale. (165)

True Riches

Possession makes not rich. He is a wealthy man
Who can all that he has, lose without hurt or pain. (167)

Two Ways of Losing Oneself

How can I lose myself? Oh, yes, it's sad, in death.
If you are lost in God, then I declare you blest. (170)

In the Sea, All Drops Become the Sea

The drop becomes the sea when it the sea has reached;
The soul does God become, if once in God received. (171)

In the Sea a Little Drop Is Also the Sea

All in the sea is sea, even the tiniest drop;
Tell me, which holy soul will not be God in God? (173)

Union with God Is Simple

Man, you can see yourself with God much quicker one,
Than opening an eye; will it, and it is done. (175)

BOOK SIX

The Foolish Seeker

If something you do seek and think God is not all,
For all eternity you pass up God and all. (188)

Security Causes Loss

Stand, fast, keep vigil, pray; wrapped in security
Many a man has lost bliss in eternity. (201)

One Should Flee Three Things

Child, shun, avoid, and flee wine, woman, and the night;
Many a man they have of body and soul deprived. (202)

A Dark Heart Cannot See

Never neglect the fire; if lamps are not aburning,
Who shall then greet the groom, when He will be returning?[7] (203)

Externals Are Worthless

What is outside yourself does not convey much worth;
Clothes do not make the man, the saddle not the horse. (209)

It Is Foolish Not To Act according To One's Belief

Christian, are you a fool? You trust eternity
Yet cling with body and soul to temporality. (212)

The Secret Noble Birth

Of God I have been born, begotten in His Son,
Sanctified by the Spirit, thus has my crown been won. (233)

The Working of the Blessed Trinity

The Son redeemeth us, the Spirit vivifies,
The Father omnipotent will make us divinized. (234)

---

7. Allusion to the parable of the five wise and the five foolish virgins (Mt 25:1ff.).

ANGELUS SILESIUS

A Sigh to God

God takes up sense and spirit, He is a mighty stream;
Oh, if I only were wholly submerged in Him. (239)

The Wise Man's Never Alone

The wise man's never alone; if no one walks with him,
He has for company the master of all things. (242)

Not To See God Is To See Nothing

You travel wide and far to scout and see and search;
If God you fail to see, you have nothing observed. (248)

The Wise Man Receives Only from God

The wise man's proud of heart. If you a gift him send,
He never will accept, unless it's from God's hand. (254)

How One Becomes Wise

If you want to be wise, God within comprehend,
You first must burn away your own concupiscence. (258)

Index to Introduction

INDEX

Index to Text

Other Volumes in this Series